An Essay on the Life of the

Honourable Major-General Israel Putnam

DAVID HUMPHREYS

ISRAEL PUTNAM

AN

ESSAY ON THE LIFE

OF THE

HONOURABLE MAJOR-GENERAL

ISRAEL PUTNAM

Addressed to the State Society of the Cincinnati
in Connecticut and Published by Their Order

DAVID HUMPHREYS

Foreword by William C. Dowling

LIBERTY FUND

Indianapolis

© 2000 Liberty Fund, Inc. All rights reserved
Illustrations by Corbis-Bettmann

| 04 | 03 | 02 | 01 | 00 | C | 5 | 4 | 3 | 2 | 1 |
| 04 | 03 | 02 | 01 | 00 | P | 5 | 4 | 3 | 2 | 1 |

Library of Congress Cataloging-in-Publication Data
Humphreys, David, 1752–1818.
An essay on the life of the Honourable Major-General Israel Putnam:
addressed to the State Society of the Cincinnati in Connecticut and published
by their order/David Humphreys; foreword by William C. Dowling.
p.   cm.
Includes index.
Contents: Letter to the Honourable Colonel Jeremiah Wadsworth—An
essay on the life of the Honourable Major-General Israel Putnam—An oration
on the political situation of the United States of America in the year 1789.
ISBN 0-86597-262-1 (alk. paper)—ISBN 0-86597-263-x (pbk. : alk. paper)
1. Putnam, Israel, 1718–1790.   2. Generals—United States—Biography.
3. United States. Army—Biography.   4. United States—History—
Revolution, 1775–1783—Campaigns.   5. United States—History—French
and Indian War, 1755–1763—Campaigns.   6. United States—History—
Revolution, 1775–1783—Personal narratives.   7. United States—History—
French and Indian War, 1755–1763—Personal narratives.   I. Title.
E207.P9 H9 2000   973.3′3′092—dc21
[B]   99-049398

Liberty Fund, Inc.
8335 Allison Pointe Trail, Suite 300
Indianapolis, Indiana 46250–1684

Contents

Foreword, ix

A Note on the Text, xxiii

Letter to the Honourable Colonel
Jeremiah Wadsworth, 1

An Essay on the Life of the Honourable
Major-General Israel Putnam, 5

An Oration on the Political Situation of the
United States of America in the Year 1789, 127

Index, 141

D avid Humphreys, author of *An Essay on the Life of the Honourable Major-General Israel Putnam,* is today remembered less as a writer than as a historical personage. As principal aide-de-camp to Putnam and subsequently to George Washington, Humphreys passed through the darkest hours of the American Revolution, when a tiny, ragged, sickly band of citizen soldiers struggled to keep up the pretense that they could oppose the greatest military power in Europe. He was present at Yorktown when, with the aid of a French fleet, the same army miraculously brought about the surrender of British forces under Cornwallis. In a signal demonstration of the regard in which Humphreys was always held by his Commander-in-Chief, he was chosen by Washington to carry the surrendered British colors to Congress in Philadelphia. After the war Humphreys pursued a distinguished career as diplomatic representative of the new United States in Portugal and Spain. He spent the closing years of his life as a successful manufacturer and energetic promoter of American self-sufficiency in manufactures in his home state of Connecticut.

The irony is that Humphreys thought of his contribution to American literature as being as significant as any of his achievements in war or diplomacy. A member of the talented group of Yale undergraduates now known as the Connecticut Wits, who among them would produce such notable examples of early

American writing as *M'Fingal* (John Trumbull), *The Triumph of Infidelity* and *Greenfield Hill* (Timothy Dwight), and *The Vision of Columbus* (Joel Barlow), Humphreys worked steadily in the interludes of his career on a body of verse celebrating the young American republic as an embodiment of what, in classical republican political theory, is called *virtus:* simplicity, hardihood, a willingness to live for the community rather than for narrow or egoistic self-interest. For Humphreys, it was *virtus* that explained the rise of republican Rome in the ancient world—before, as the victim of its own success, it had sunk inevitably into luxury and corruption—and it was *virtus* that explained the victory of the American colonies over England.

Yet Humphreys's poetic talents were modest, and today his poetry is of interest only to specialists in early American literature. His one work of lasting value was produced quickly at a historical moment when the new confederation of American states seemed to him quite literally to be disintegrating. This work was *An Essay on the Life of the Honourable Major-General Israel Putnam*. The word "essay" in the title, retaining its older meaning of "trial" or "attempt," was meant simply to signal the occasional nature of Humphreys's short biography, which he composed for the Connecticut Society of the Cincinnati in 1787, when it was not possible for him to be present to address the Society's annual meeting. The significance of the *Life of Putnam* derives from Humphreys's attempt in it to epitomize, in the form of a short Plutarchan biography, the myth of *virtus* or civic virtue that he believed to be at the heart of the American Revolution.

For Americans of the revolutionary generation, nothing more powerfully summarized the myth of *virtus* than the story of Cincinnatus, the retired Roman consul who had been called from his plough to lead the Roman army against an invading

enemy, and who, having won the victory, immediately surrendered his power and returned to the plough. Here were all the
elements that led so many eighteenth-century Americans to
identify their own state with that of the early Roman republic:
an agrarian society uncorrupted by luxury, a life of field and
vineyard still close to the miraculously regenerative powers of
the earth, a moral simplicity that viewed the glittering attrac-
tions of public or political life—power, wealth, influence—as
no more than unwholesome delusions. Our meaning of *dictator,*
which summons up the Hitlers and Stalins of the modern age,
suggests how unimaginably far we have traveled from that memory of mythic simplicity. For to the early Romans, a dictator was
an honored and trusted leader to whom the people temporarily
granted, as they did to Cincinnatus, absolute power in a time of
national peril. This is the early Rome, in short, of Livy's history,
or Rollin's or Goldsmith's Roman histories, or Dyer's *The Ruins
of Rome,* a poem that would have been familiar to most readers
of Humphreys's *Life of Putnam:*

> From the plough
> Rose her dictators; fought, o'ercame, returned,
> Yes, to the plough returned, and hailed their peers;
> For then no private pomp, no household state,
> The public only swelled the generous breast.

Humphreys's Israel Putnam is an American Cincinnatus, as
brave and honest a man, as Humphreys says in his dedicatory
letter to Jeremiah Wadsworth, as ever America produced. Thus
it is, for instance, that when we first meet Putnam he is a simple
yeoman with no more education than is needed by a farmer in
a nation of farmers, but with native qualities of fearlessness and
integrity that make him a natural leader. This is the Putnam
who goes down into the darksome den of a ferocious she-wolf—

in Humphreys's narrative a naturalized version of the hero's journey to the underworld—to reemerge as a half-mythic figure to
his neighbors. It is the Putnam who displays an inexhaustible
bravery and resourcefulness in the Seven Years' War, and who
survives a brutal Indian captivity in Canada to return to his home
in Connecticut. It is, finally, the hero whose circumstances are
identical with those of Cincinnatus when news comes of the
shots fired at Concord and Lexington. Putnam, Humphreys
solemnly reports, "who was plowing when he heard the news,
left his plough in the middle of the field" to set off instantly for
the theater of action.

The *Life of Israel Putnam* divides into two halves, the first being largely taken up with Putnam's deeds in the Seven Years'
War—the "French and Indian War" of American history—the
second being devoted to his role in the American Revolution.
The first half, it is sometimes said, is closer to romance than to
biography or history. This is especially true if by "romance" one
means Hawthorne's sense of the strangeness of an America that
is still trackless wilderness, with a mysterious world of wild
beasts and hostile Indians lurking just beyond the feeble glow
of light cast by isolated settlements. It is no wonder that James
Fenimore Cooper would when writing *The Last of the Mohicans*
turn to the *Life of Putnam* for details of frontier war, for innumerable scenes in Humphreys's early pages—scalpings, eviscerations, Indians howling around the pyres where captives are
burning alive—belong to a familiar mythology of the early
American frontier.

The usual reason given for the resemblance of this portion of
the *Life of Putnam* to fable or romance is that Humphreys was
working from anecdotes sent to him by Dr. Albigence Waldo, a
former army surgeon who had interviewed Putnam at length
about his experiences in the French and Indian War, and who

was therefore able to provide a sort of oral history of events as Putnam remembered them. It is true enough that Humphreys was working from these materials—a footnote in the *Life* takes an early opportunity to thank Waldo for his help—but it is also true, as Humphreys makes clear, that he had himself gone over much of this same ground with Putnam, taking the trouble to check or verify various points. Yet the atmosphere of romance, an ethos closer to myth or heroic legend than mere factual narrative, survives unaltered.

The reason why this is so takes us to the heart of the literary and cultural significance of the *Life of Putnam.* For while Humphreys is always interested in telling the truth—in the opening pages of the *Life* he is quite hard on previous writers who have circulated "fables and marvellous stories" about the heroes of the Revolution—he is also consciously writing within a Plutarchan tradition that takes the truth about a biographical hero to be moral rather than circumstantial or factual. The *Life of Putnam* is meant to be, in the phrase coined by John Dryden in a famous essay on Plutarch, philosophy teaching by example. This is what Humphreys has in mind, for instance, when he states, early in the *Life,* that his ends will have been served if he produces in his American readers a desire to imitate the "domestic, manly and heroic virtues" of Israel Putnam.

The point of Plutarchan biography, still the commanding model in that classically oriented age, is to give back to the community a sustaining image of its own deepest values in the personality of the hero.

Consider, from this perspective, the likelihood that Putnam, like Cincinnatus in the episode from Livy, should have been actually plowing his field when news of the battle at Concord and Lexington arrived. To modern ears, conditioned by nearly two centuries of the "scientific" history that began with Ranke's dictum that the historian's task is to recreate the past *wie es eigent-lich gewesen,* the implausibility of such a story is nearly over-whelming. But, to Dr. Albigence Waldo, taking down Putnam's stories of his earlier adventures, or to David Humphreys, asking his old commander to recall the events that had preceded his important role in the American Revolution, nothing could be more natural than that an aging warrior, brought up on stories of Cincinnatus and Regulus and Horatio at the bridge, should remember his own story in such terms. To set the story down in the way it is told is, therefore, simply to assent to the truth that a society lives by its myths, and that myth at a certain level func-tions as something very like collective or cultural memory.

The spirit of the first half of the *Life of Putnam* is nowhere better caught than in an episode in Humphreys's poem *On the Happiness of America,* written immediately after the Revolution when Humphreys, then abroad in Europe, was reflecting on his society from a certain idealizing distance. The scene in the poem is an American homestead in winter, the wind howling and the snow drifting along the roads. The crops have been har-vested, the cattle are warm in their stalls, and now family and neighbors have gathered around the cheerful blaze of the hearth to, as Humphreys says, indulge in tales, news, politics, and mirth. The tale they hear on this occasion is told by an "old war-rior, grown a village sage," and it begins with his early adven-tures and proceeds to the Revolutionary War battles in which he took part—"The big bomb bursts, the fragments scatter'd round"—until, at the last, he pulls aside his shirt to reveal his scars. The children, listening wide-eyed, suddenly understand that this fireside tale is their own story, that this tiny community around the hearth is able peacefully to gather only because oth-ers have gone forth to distant fields of battle willing to die "in freedom's name."

The second half of the *Life of Putnam* is, in the conventional sense, more soberly "historical," more concerned with dates and events and the movements of British and American troops in various campaigns. The new factor introduced into the narrative is, of course, Humphreys's own first-person perspective, for during much of this portion of the story he was at Putnam's side as events unfolded, and even later when he served as Washington's aide-de-camp he was continuously aware of Putnam's day-to-day movements. Yet the shift toward a more matter-of-fact perspective is not altogether owing to Humphreys's participation in the story, for what he understands as having occurred is that American society, under the disintegrative pressures of war and competing political loyalties, has begun to lose that quality of spiritual coherence that had sustained a younger Israel Putnam in a sort of natural or spontaneous heroism.

A sense that the onset of the Revolutionary War marked the collapse of a mythic dimension in American life, the end of a period when ordinary men and women had, all unawares, moved about the world as though in an atmosphere of song or legend, is something one encounters repeatedly in the writing of this period. One gets a strong sense of it in, for instance, the letters exchanged between John and Abigail Adams during his absence at the Continental Congress, with both husband and wife aware that they have somehow become characters in a momentous story in which people like themselves, ordinary enough souls in any other epoch, have been given a momentous role to play. This is what Humphreys is trying to get at when, in the *Life of Putnam*, he remarks that his own generation has "fallen upon an era singularly prolific in extraordinary personages, and dignified by splendid events." More particularly, this is what gives full meaning to Humphreys's declaration that Putnam, whom he has by implication chosen as biographical hero for this reason, "seems to have been formed on purpose for the age in which he lived."

The division between the two halves of the *Life of Putnam* is thus meant to signal Humphreys's own sense of a chasm or rupture in the continuity of American history, the loss of a world in which someone like Israel Putnam could appear as a Plutarchan hero because he was, in a manner of speaking, dwelling within a Plutarchan society, a world in certain essential respects resembling that of ancient Athens or early republican Rome. In the second half of the *Life of Putnam,* it is this sense of an all-sustaining *virtus,* a moral medium able to make heroes and heroines out of otherwise ordinary souls, that has vanished. The outbreak of the Revolutionary War represents, in Humphreys's narrative, a fall into history-as-such, a world of power and intrigue and competing interests that is a very old story to the corrupt and cynical states of Europe, but whose appearance on this side of the Atlantic marks the vanishing of what Humphreys once calls the golden age of "equality, innocence, and security" into which Americans of Putnam's generation had been born.

The obvious tension that works to dissolve the spiritual coherence of American society once war has broken out is, of course, that between Whigs and Loyalists, those who support American independence versus those who remain loyal to King and Parliament. But this tension is backlighted in the second half of Humphreys's *Life of Putnam* by the more tragic dissolution of American society into narrow self-interest or atomistic egoism, a new Hobbesian social reality in which people are avidly learning how to disregard the interests of the community in favor of this or that specific advantage to themselves. In Humphreys's telling of the story, the British forces ranged against Washington's tiny army are only the visible enemy. The invisible enemy is the growing sway of self-interest, the most foreboding symptom of which is that so many Americans during this time of trial profess support for liberty while leaving the soldiers of their own army without food, clothing, shelter, supplies, or pay that could be sent to their families.

Thus it is that, in the second half of the *Life of Putnam,* the themes of *virtus* and Plutarchan heroism are transposed from the Putnam who went down into the cave to fight the wolf, the Putnam who battled fire in a frontier barracks until the skin burned off his hands, and the Putnam who went out as a solitary scout against ferocious Indians, to what Humphreys calls the patriot army—the small band of militia, minutemen, and volunteers who remain with Washington through the long dark winter of the revolutionary struggle, sustained by little more than a dogged loyalty to their leaders and their cause. As a larger-than-life Putnam is the hero of the first half of the biographical story, so the hero of the second half is this ragged band of largely anonymous souls, a tiny community of *virtus* that symbolizes collectively what the younger Putnam had symbolized as an individual. It is an army which, as Humphreys states,

Having vindicated the rights of human nature, and established the independence of a new empire, merited and obtained the glorious distinction of the patriot army—the patriot army, whose praises for their fortitude in adversity, bravery in battle, moderation in conquest, perseverance in supporting the cruel extremities of hunger and nakedness without a murmur or sigh, as well as for their magnanimity in retiring to civil life, at the moment of victory, with their arms in their hands, and without any just compensation for their services, will only cease to be celebrated when time shall exist no more.

The story of the patriot army in the American Revolution is, therefore, the subject of the second half of the *Life of Putnam*. Parts of the story are merely entertaining, as when Putnam, whose forces in his winter encampment at Princeton have been reduced to a mere 50 men, is compelled by circumstances to permit a British officer to visit his headquarters. The stratagems through which he convinces the officer that his troops actually number in the thousands—by putting candles in the windows of Nassau Hall and every vacant house in the town of Princeton, and by marching the same 50 men around all night in detachments of five, ten, and twenty—borders on comedy, but Humphreys never lets the reader forget that such episodes mask an underlying desperation. For a large garrison of British troops is camped a mere 15 miles away in New Brunswick. Should the British learn just how few soldiers Putnam actually commands at Princeton, or how few Washington has a few miles away at Morristown, or how little the Congress has done to clothe or supply even these tiny forces, the American Revolution would, the reader understands, be over in a week.

An even grimmer note is struck as the Revolution comes, against all odds, to a victorious close, and it becomes clear that the same Congress that has refused to support its army in the field is going to allow it to disband without being paid. Men who have given up everything, who have risked their lives and left their families to subsist on the charity of their neighbors, will be sent home destitute, without money even to pay for seed for next season's planting. A foreshadowing of this bitter situation occurs near the very end of the *Life of Putnam*, when the Connecticut brigade then under Putnam's command, having brooded all winter on the ingratitude of a nation that has been willing to starve them before sending them forth to die in battle, decides to march on Hartford to demand its back pay from the General Assembly. Putnam saves the day on this occasion by getting early word of the mutiny, riding into camp at the last moment, and making a stirring speech on duty and patriotism. "You have behaved like men so far—all the world is full of your praises," he declares—and orders the troops, chastened, back to barracks, but not before we have seen that he understands and sympathizes with his soldiers' anger.

At the very end of the *Life,* Putnam suffers a stroke and loses the power of his limbs on one side of his body, and so is sent into unwilling and premature retirement on his Connecticut farm while others play out the final scenes of the Revolutionary drama. Yet, in a way, this is the most poignant section of the biographical story, as Putnam becomes a living symbol of the patriot army, all those badly clothed and poorly fed men who have kept alive the spark of liberty while thousands of others— voicing patriotic sentiments—have gone about their business, very often at considerable profit to themselves. We are meant to see, at this point—or, more precisely, the original American readers of the *Life of Putnam* were meant to see—that in extreme circumstances patriotism is simply another name for gratitude, a perpetual awareness of the moral debt owed by any community to those by whose selflessness or sacrifice it has been sustained.

For Humphreys and his fellow Federalists, the paradox of the American Revolution is that it has been carried out in the name of republican government, which those raised on Aristotle and Polybius understood to be perennially threatened with the dissolution of society into selfishness. The glory of republican government, from the *polis* of ancient Greece to the rise of Rome, had been that it awarded to every citizen a role in determining the fate of his community. The corresponding danger is that men given individual rights may begin to think exclusively in terms of individual interests, which in the *Life of Putnam*, especially in the relation between America and its forlorn army of patriot soldiers, is seen as a form of moral blindness. The *Life* ends with a letter written by Washington to Israel Putnam on his Connecticut farm. Its ostensible subject is the matter of Putnam's back pay as a Major General. Its real subject is the question whether the America for which he and Putnam and their fellow soldiers have risked everything has turned out to be, after all, worth the sacrifice:

> While I contemplate the greatness of the object for which we have contended and felicitate you on the happy issue of our toils and labours . . . I lament that you should feel the ungrateful returns of a country, in whose service you have exhausted your bodily strength, and expended the vigour of a youthful constitution. I wish, however, that your expectations of returning liberality may be verified. I have a hope they may—but should they not, your case will not be a singular one. *Ingratitude has been experienced in all ages*, and REPUBLICS, *in particular, have ever been famed for the exercise of that unnatural and* SORDID VICE.

In the years following the Treaty of Paris, the dark foreboding so audible in Washington's letter to Putnam comes to seem all too prophetic. For these are the years during which the new United States nearly disintegrate into a mere collection of squabbling petty republics, each attempting to gain advantage over the others on such matters as impost duties and tariffs. They are the years during which worthless paper currency, widely manipulated by speculators to the ruin of many an honest tradesman or farmer, is circulated by apparently oblivious state governments. Preeminently, they are the years during which the grievances of the veterans of Washington and Putnam's patriot army issue in something very close to civil war, most spectacularly in Shays's Rebellion in western Massachusetts. It is in this downward spiral into anarchy, a relieved Humphreys will later say in his *Oration on the Political Situation of the United States in 1789*, in which the new United States touched on its very "hour of humiliation."

The *Oration*, which represents at once a commentary on and a cautiously optimistic coda to the *Life of Putnam*, is, like the *Life*, addressed to Humphreys's beloved Society of the Cincinnati, the organization formed by Washington's officers in the last weeks before Congress would send them, along with their unpaid troops, back to their homes. In form, it is simply a grateful chronicle of the events leading to the Constitutional Convention in Philadelphia, the adoption of the new Constitution by the eleven states needed to put it into force, and the election of George Washington as the new chief executive. In spirit, however, it is a hymn of praise, a celebration of the unexpected return of *virtus* to a nation that even Washington himself had once thought to be on the verge of disintegration. "Can we contemplate a work so vast in its import," asks Humphreys, "and so wonderfully effected—not by violence and bloodshed, but by deliberation and consent—without exclaiming in rapturous admiration, behold a new thing under the sun?"

Yet even amidst the rapture there is a note of bleak moral realism. Human nature has in all ages been impatient of restraint, and no form of government can guarantee that the spirit of *virtus*—a care for the life of the whole as well as one's own interests—will continue to sustain any historical society. Events may well yet prove, as Humphreys soberly acknowledges, "that no wall of words, that no mound of parchment, can be so formed as to stand against the sweeping torrent of boundless ambition on the one side, aided by the sapping current of corrupted morals on the other." No matter what occurs in the future, however, nothing can take away from Americans the shining moment in their history in which men like George Washington and Israel Putnam walked in the light of day, and when every week brought events that were, as Humphreys declares, the delight and admiration of the world. It is as a vivid memorial of that moment that the *Life of Israel Putnam* survives today.

William C. Dowling
Princeton, New Jersey

A Note on the Text

The texts of both the *Life of Israel Putnam* and the *Oration on the Political Situation of the United States in 1789* have been taken from the last-published edition of *The Miscellaneous Works of David Humphreys*, printed in New York in 1804. In keeping with the principles governing Liberty Fund editions, textual alterations have been kept to a bare minimum.

One alteration is the standardization of variant spellings for several common and proper nouns. On the same principle, I have replaced the archaic use of *our's* with *ours* in the few instances where it occurred in the 1804 text. One obvious misprint—*killed on the sport* for *killed on the spot*, page 37—has been corrected.

An Essay on the Life of the
Honourable Major-General Israel Putnam

Letter to the Honourable
Colonel Jeremiah Wadsworth

To the
Hon. Col. Jeremiah Wadsworth,
President of the State Society of the Cincinnati
in Connecticut, &c.

My dear Sir,

Unavoidable absence will prevent me from performing the
grateful task assigned me by the State Society of the Cincinnati
on the fourth day of July next. Though I cannot personally address them, I wish to demonstrate, by some token of affectionate remembrance, the sense I entertain of the honour they have
more than once conferred upon me by their suffrages.

Meditating in what manner to accomplish this object, it occurred to me, that an attempt to preserve the actions of General
Putnam, in the archives of our State Society, would be acceptable to its members, as they had all served with great satisfaction
under his immediate orders. An essay on the life of a person so
elevated in military rank, and so conversant in extraordinary
scenes, could not be destitute of amusement and instruction,
and would possess the advantage of presenting for imitation a
respectable model of public and private virtues.

I

General Putnam is universally acknowledged to have been as brave and as honest a man as ever America produced; but the distinguishing features of his character, and the particular transactions of his life, are but imperfectly known. He seems to have been formed on purpose for the age in which he lived. His native courage, unshaken integrity, and established reputation as a soldier, were necessary in the early stages of our opposition to the designs of Great-Britain, and gave unbounded confidence to our troops in their first conflicts in the field of battle.

The enclosed manuscript justly claims indulgence for its venial errors, as it is the first effort in Biography that has been made on this continent. The attempt, I am conscious, is laudable, whatever may be the failure in point of execution.

I am happy to find the Society of the Cincinnati is now generally regarded in a favourable manner. Mankind, with few exceptions, are disposed to do justice to the motives on which it was founded. For ourselves, we can never recall to mind the occasion, without feeling the most tender emotions of friendship and sensibility. At the dissolution of the army, when we retired to separate walks of life, from the toils of a successful war, in which we had been associated during a very important part of our lives, the pleasing idea, and the fond hope of meeting once a year, *which gave birth to our fraternal institution,* were necessary consolations to sooth the pangs that tore our bosoms at the melancholy hour of parting. When our hands touched, perhaps for the last time, and our tongues refused to perform their office in bidding farewell, heaven witnessed and approved the purity of our intentions in the ardour of our affections. May we persevere in the union of our friendship, and the exertion of our benevolence; regardless of the censures of jealous suspicion, which charges our designs with selfishness, and ascribes our actions to improper motives; while we realize sentiments of a nobler nature in our anniversary festivities, and our hearts dilate with an honest joy, in opening the hand of beneficence to the indigent widow and unprotected orphan of our departed friends.

I pray you, my dear Sir, to present my most respectful compliments to the members of the Society, and to assure them, on my part, that whensoever it shall be in my power, I shall esteem it the felicity of my life to attend their anniversaries.

I have the honour to be,

    With sentiments of the highest consideration and esteem,

    Your most obedient and most humble servant,

                D. HUMPHREYS

Mount-Vernon, in Virginia,
June 4, 1788

An Essay on the
Life of General Putnam

T o treat of recent transactions and persons still living, is always a delicate, and frequently a thankless office. Yet, while the partiality of friends, or the malignity of enemies, decides with rashness on every delineation of character, or recital of circumstances, a consolation remains, that distant nations, and remoter ages, free from the influence of prejudice or passion, will judge with impartiality, and appreciate with justice. We have fallen upon an era singularly prolific in extraordinary personages, and dignified by splendid events. Much is expected from the selections of the judicious biographer, as well as from the labours of the faithful historian. Whatever prudential reasons may now occur to postpone the portrait of our own times, the difficulties which oppose themselves to the execution, instead of being diminished, will increase with the lapse of years. Every day will extinguish some life that was dear to fame, and obliterate the memorial of some deed which would have constituted the delight and admiration of the world.

So transient and indistinguishable are the traits of character, so various and inexplicable the springs of action, so obscure and perishable the remembrance of human affairs, that, unless attempts are made to sketch the picture, while the present generation is living, the likeness will be for ever lost, or only preserved by a vague recollection; disguised, perhaps, by the whimsical colourings of a creative imagination.

It will, doubtless, hereafter be an object of regret, that those who, having themselves been conspicuous actors on the theatre of public life, and who, in conjunction with a knowledge of facts, possess abilities to paint those characters, and describe those events which, during the progress of the American Revolution, interested and astonished mankind, should feel an insuperable reluctance to assume the task—a task which, if executed with fidelity, must, from the dignity of its subject, become grateful to the patriots of all nations, and profitable in example to the remotest posterity. Equally severe will be the mortification of contemplating the reveries and fictions which have been substituted by hacknied writers in the place of historical facts. Nor should we suppress our indignation against that class of professional authors, who, placed in the vale of penury and obscurity, at an immense distance from the scenes of action, and all opportunities of acquiring the necessary documents, with insufferable effrontery, obtrude their fallacious and crude performances on a credulous public. Did the result of their lucubrations terminate only in relieving their own distresses, or gratifying their individual vanity, it might be passed in silent contempt. But the effect is extensive, permanent, and pernicious. The lie,* however improbable or monstrous, which has once assumed the semblance of truth, by being often repeated

---

* The writer had here particularly in his eye the Rhapsody palmed upon the public, under the name of a history, by a certain Frenchman, called D'Auberteiul: Perhaps so much falsehood, folly, and calumny was never before accumulated in a single performance.

with minute and plausible particulars, is, at length, so thoroughly established, as to obtain universal credit, defy contradiction, and frustrate every effort of refutation. Such is the mischief, such are the unhappy consequences on the bewildered mind, that the reader has no alternative, but to become the dupe of his credulity, or distrust the veracity of almost all human testimony. After having long been the sport of fiction, he will, perhaps, probably run into the opposite extreme, and give up all confidence in the annals of ancient as well as modern times; and thus the easy believer of fine fables and marvelous stories will find, at last, his historical faith change to scepticism, and end in infidelity.

The numerous errors and falsehoods relative to the birth and achievements of Major-General Putnam, which have (at a former period) been circulated with assiduity on both sides of the Atlantic, and the uncertainty which appeared to prevail with respect to his real character,* first produced the resolution of

---

* The following lines are extracted from a Poem, entitled, "The Prospect of America," written by the late ingenious Dr. Ladd.

Hail Putnam! hail thou venerable name!
Though dark oblivion threats thy mighty fame,
It threats in vain—for long shalt thou be known,
Who first in virtue and in battle shone,
When fourscore years had blanch'd thy laurel'd head,
Strong in thine age, the flame of war was spread.

On which Dr. Ladd made this note:

The brave Putnam seems to have been almost obscured amidst the glare of succeeding worthies; but his early and gallant services entitle him to an everlasting remembrancy.

Other bards have also asserted the glory of this venerable veteran. In the first

writing this essay on his life, and induced the Editor to obtain*
materials from that hero himself. If communications of such
authenticity, if personal intimacy as an aid-de-camp to that
General, or if subsequent military employments, which afforded
access to sources† of intelligence not open to others, give the

---

concise review of the principal American heroes who signalized themselves in
the last war, the same character is thus represented:

> There stood stern Putnam, seam'd with many a scar,
> The veteran honours of an early war.
> The Vision of Columbus, Book V.

* The Editor seizes, with eagerness, an opportunity of acknowledging his
obligations to Dr. Albigence Waldo, who was so obliging as to commit to
writing many anecdotes, communicated to him by General Putnam in the
course of the present year.

† A multitude of proofs might be produced to demonstrate that military
facts cannot always be accurately known but by the Commander in Chief, and
his confidential officers. The Marquis de Chastelleux (whose opportunity to
acquire genuine information, respecting those parts of the American war
which he hath casually mentioned, was better than that of any other writer)
gives an account of a grand forage which General Heath ordered to be made
towards King's-bridge in the autumn of 1780. The Marquis, who was present
when the detachment marched, and to whom General Heath showed the orders that were given to General Stark, the commanding officer of the expedition, observes, that he had never seen, in manuscript or print, more perti-
nent instructions. Now the fact is, that this detachment, under the pretext of
a forage, was intended by the Commander in Chief to cooperate with the
main army in an attempt against the enemy's posts on York Island; and that
General Heath himself was then ignorant of the real design. The Commander
in Chief spent a whole campaign in ripening this project. Boats, mounted on
travelling carriages, were kept constantly with the army. The Marquis de la
Fayette, at the head of the light infantry, was to have made the attack in the
night on Fort Washington. The period chosen for this enterprize was the very
time when the army were to break up their camp, and march into winter quarters; so that the Commander in Chief, moving in the dusk of the evening,

8

writer any advantages, the unbiassed mind will decide how far they exculpate him from the imputations of that officiousness, ignorance and presumption, which, in others, have been reprehended with severity. He only wishes that a premature and unfavourable construction may not be formed of his motive or object. Should this essay have any influence in correcting mistakes, or rescuing from oblivion the actions of that distinguished veteran; should it create an emulation to copy his domestic, manly

---

would have been on the banks of the Hudson, with his whole force, to have supported the attack. The cautious manner in which the cooperation on the part of the troops sent by General Heath, on the pretended forage, was to have been conducted, will be understood from the following secret instructions.

To Brigadier-General STARK.
Head Quarters, Passaic-Falls, Nov. 21, 1780.
SIR,
    Colonel Humphreys, one of my Aids-de-camp, is charged by me, with orders of a private and particular nature, which he is to deliver to you, and which you are to obey. He will inform you of the necessity of this mode of communication.
I am, Sir, &c,

G. WASHINGTON.

To Lieutenant-Colonel DAVID HUMPHREYS, A. D. Camp.
SIR,
    You are immediately to proceed to West-Point, and communicate the business committed to you, in confidence, to Major-General Heath, and to no other person whatsoever; from thence you will repair to the detachment at the White-Plains, on Friday next, taking measures to prevent their leaving that place before you get to them. And, in the course of the succeeding night, you may inform the commanding officer of the enterprize in contemplation against the enemy's posts on York Island.
    As the troops are constantly to lie on their arms, no previous notice should be given; but they may be put in motion precisely at four o'clock, and commence a slow and regular march to King's-bridge, until they shall discover, or be informed of the concerted signals being made—when the march must be

9

and heroic virtues; or should it prompt some more skilful hand to portray the illustrious group of patriots, sages, and heroes, who have guided our councils, fought our battles, and adorned the memorable epocha of independence, it will be an ample compensation for the trouble, and excite a consolatory reflection through every vicissitude of life.

---

pressed with the greatest rapidity. Parties of horse should be sent forward to keep a look out for the signals.

Although the main body ought to be kept compact, patrols of horse and light parties might be sent towards East and West Chester: and upon the signals being discovered, Sheldon's regiment, and the Connecticut State troops (which may also be put in motion as soon as the orders can be communicated after four o'clock) should be pushed forward to intercept any of the enemy who may attempt to gain Frog's Neck, and to cut off the Refugee-corps at Morissania. A few men, with some address, may spread such an alarm as to prevent an attempt of the enemy to retreat to Frog's Neck, from an apprehension of surrounding parties.

You will communicate these instructions to the commanding officer of the detachment, who, upon his approach to King's-bridge, will receive orders from me as early as possible.

Should the signals not be discovered, the troops will halt at least six miles from the bridge, until further intelligence can be obtained.

The absolute necessity of the most perfect secrecy is the occasion of communicating my orders through this channel.

Given at Head-Quarters, Passaic-Falls, this 22d day of Nov. 1780.

G. WASHINGTON.

Never was a plan better arranged: and never did circumstances promise more sure or complete success. The British were not only unalarmed, but our own troops were likewise entirely misguided in their expectations. The accidental intervention of some vessels prevented, at this time, the attempt; which was more than once resumed afterwards. Notwithstanding this favourite project was not ultimately effected, it was evidently not less bold in conception or feasible in accomplishment, than that attempted so successfully at Trenton, or

ISRAEL PUTNAM, who, through a regular gradation of promotion, became the senior Major-General in the army of the
United States, and next in rank to General Washington, was
born at Salem, in the Province (now State) of Massachusetts,
on the 7th day of January, 1718. His father, Captain Joseph Putnam, was the son of Mr. John Putnam, who, with two brothers,
came from the south of England, and were among the first settlers of Salem.

When we thus behold a person, from the humble walks of
life, starting unnoticed in the career of fame, and, by an undevi-
ating progress through a life of honour, arriving at the highest
dignity in the state, curiosity is strongly excited, and philosophy
loves to trace the path of glory from the cradle of obscurity to
the summit of elevation.

Although our ancestors, the first settlers of this land, amidst
the extreme pressure of poverty and danger, early instituted
schools for the education of youth designed for the learned pro-
fessions, yet it was thought sufficient to instruct those destined
to labour on the earth, in reading, writing, and such rudiments
of arithmetic as might be requisite for keeping the accounts of
their little transactions with each other. Few farmers' sons had

---

than that which was brought to so glorious an issue in the successful siege of
York-Town.

It is true, the Marquis de Chastelleux, whose professional knowledge and
fountainhead intelligence have enabled him to describe several actions better
than they are elsewhere described, speaks in this instance of an ulterior object;
and says, that secrets were preserved more inviolably in the American than in
the French army. His words are:

> C'est que le secret est garde tres exactement a l'armee Americaine; peu
> de personnes ont part a la confiance du Chef, et en general on y parle
> moins que dans les armees Francoises des operations de la guerre, et de
> ce que l'on appelle chez nous *les Nouvelles.*

more advantages, none less. In this state of mediocrity it was the lot of young Putnam to be placed. His early instruction was not considerable, and the active scenes of life in which he was afterwards engaged, prevented the opportunity of great literary improvement. His numerous original letters, though deficient in scholastic accuracy, always display the goodness of his heart, and frequently the strength of his native genius. He had a certain laconic mode of expression, and an unaffected epigrammatic turn, which characterised most of his writings.

To compensate partially for the deficiency of education (though nothing can remove or counterbalance the inconveniencies experienced from it in public life) he derived from his parents the source of innumerable advantages in the stamina of a vigorous constitution. Nature, liberal in bestowing on him bodily strength, hardiness, and activity, was by no means parsimonious in mental endowments. While we leave the qualities of the understanding to be developed in the process of life, it may not be improper, in this place, to designate some of the circumstances which were calculated to distinguish him afterwards as a partizan officer.

Courage, enterprize, activity, and perseverance were the first characteristics of his mind. There is a kind of mechanical courage, the offspring of pride, habit, or discipline, that may push a coward not only to perform his duty, but even to venture on acts of heroism. Putnam's courage was of a different species. It was ever attended with a serenity of soul, a clearness of conception, a degree of self-possession, and a superiority to all the vicissitudes of fortune, entirely distinct from any thing that can be produced by the ferment of blood, and flutter of spirits; which, not unfrequently, precipitate men to action, when stimulated by intoxication or some other transient exhilaration. The heroic character, thus founded on constitution and animal spirits, cherished by education and ideas of personal freedom, confirmed by temperance and habits of exercise, was completed by the dictate of reason, the love of his country, and an invincible sense of duty. Such were the qualities and principles that enabled him to meet unappalled, the shafts of adversity, and to pass in triumph through the furnace of affliction.

His disposition was as frank and generous as his mind was fearless and independent. He disguised nothing; indeed he seemed incapable of disguise. Perhaps, in the intercourse he was ultimately obliged to have with an artful world, his sincerity, on some occasions, outwent his discretion. Although he had too much suavity in his nature to commence a quarrel, he had too much sensibility not to feel, and too much honour not to resent an intended insult. The first time he went to Boston he was insulted for his rusticity by a boy of twice his size and age; after bearing the sarcasms until his patience was worn out, he challenged, engaged, and vanquished his unmannerly antagonist, to the great diversion of a crowd of spectators. While a stripling, his ambition was to perform the labour of a man, and to excel in athletic diversions. In that rude, but masculine age, whenever the village-youth assembled on their usual occasions of festivity, pitching the bar, running, leaping, and wrestling were favourite amusements. At such gymnastic exercises (in which, during the heroic times of ancient Greece and Rome, conquest was considered as the promise of future military fame) he bore the palm from almost every ring.

Before the refinements of luxury, and the consequent increase of expenses had rendered the maintenance of a family inconvenient or burdensome in America, the sexes entered into matrimony at an early age. Competence, attainable by all, was the limit of pursuit. After the hardships of making a new settlement were overcome, and the evils of penury removed, the inhabitants enjoyed, in the lot of equality, innocence and security, scenes equally delightful with those pictured by the glowing imagination of the poets in their favourite pastoral life, or fabulous golden age. Indeed, the condition of mankind was never more enviable. Neither disparity of age and fortune, nor schemes of ambition and grandeur, nor the pride and avarice of high-minded and mercenary parents, interposed those obstacles to the union of congenial souls, which frequently in more polished society prevent, imbitter or destroy all the felicity of the connubial state. Mr. Putnam, before he attained the twenty-first year of his age, married Miss Pope, daughter of Mr. John Pope, of Salem, by whom he had ten children, seven of whom are still living. He lost the wife of his youth in 1764. Some time after he married Mrs. Gardiner, widow of the late Mr. Gardiner, of Gardiner's Island, by whom he had no issue. She died in 1777.

In the year 1739, he removed from Salem to Pomfret, an inland fertile town in Connecticut, forty miles east of Hartford. Having here purchased a considerable tract of land, he applied himself successfully to agriculture.

The first years, on a new farm, are not, however, exempt from disasters and disappointments, which can only be remedied by stubborn and patient industry. Our farmer, sufficiently occupied in building an house and barn, felling woods, making fences, sowing grain, planting orchards, and taking care of his stock, had to encounter, in turn, the calamities occasioned by drought in summer, blast in harvest, loss of cattle in winter, and the desolation of his sheep-fold by wolves. In one night he had seventy fine sheep and goats killed, besides many lambs and kids wounded. This havock was committed by a she-wolf, which, with her annual whelps, had for several years infested the vicinity. The young were commonly destroyed by the vigilance of the hunters, but the old one was too sagacious to come within reach of gun-shot: upon being closely pursued, she would generally fly to the western woods, and return the next winter with another litter of whelps.

This wolf, at length, became such an intolerable nuisance that Mr. Putnam entered into a combination with five of his neighbours to hunt alternately until they could destroy her. Two, by rotation, were to be constantly in pursuit. It was known, that, having lost the toes from one foot, by a steel-trap, she made one track shorter than the other. By this vestige the pursuers recognized, in a light snow, the route of this pernicious animal. Having followed her to Connecticut river, and found she had turned back in a direct course towards Pomfret, they immediately returned, and by ten o'clock the next morning the blood-hounds had driven her into a den, about three miles distant from the house of Mr. Putnam: The people soon collected with dogs, guns, straw, fire, and sulphur, to attack the common enemy. With this apparatus, several unsuccessful efforts were made to force her from the den. The hounds came back badly wounded, and refused to return. The smoke of blazing straw had no effect. Nor did the fumes of burnt brimstone, with which the cavern was filled, compel her to quit the retirement. Wearied with such fruitless attempts, (which had brought the time to ten o'clock at night) Mr. Putnam tried once more to make his dog enter, but in vain. He proposed to his negro man to go down into the cavern and shoot the wolf: the negro declined the hazardous service. Then it was that the master, angry at the disappointment, and declaring that he was ashamed to have a coward in his family, resolved himself to destroy the ferocious beast, lest she should escape through some unknown fissure of the rock. His neighbours strongly remonstrated against the perilous enterprize: but he, knowing that wild animals were intimidated by fire, and having provided several strips of birchbark, the only combustible material which he could obtain that would afford light in this deep and darksome cave, prepared for his descent. Having, accordingly, divested himself of his coat and waistcoat, and having a long rope fastened round his legs, by which he might be pulled back, at a concerted signal, he entered head-foremost with the blazing torch in his hand.

The aperture of the den, on the east side of a very high ledge of rocks, is about two feet square; from thence it descends obliquely fifteen feet, then running horizontally about ten more, it ascends gradually sixteen feet towards its termination. The sides of this subterraneous cavity are composed of smooth and solid rocks, which seem to have been divided from each other by some former earthquake. The top and bottom are also of stone, and the entrance, in winter, being covered with ice, is exceedingly slippery. It is in no place high enough for a man to raise himself upright, nor in any part more than three feet in width.

Having groped his passage to the horizontal part of the den, the most terrifying darkness appeared in front of the dim circle of light afforded by his torch. It was silent as the house of death. None but monsters of the desert had ever before explored this solitary mansion of horror. He, cautiously proceeding onward, came to the ascent, which he slowly mounted on his hands and knees until he discovered the glaring eye-balls of the wolf, who was sitting at the extremity of the cavern. Startled at the sight of fire, she gnashed her teeth, and gave a sullen growl. As soon as he had made the necessary discovery, he kicked the rope as a signal for pulling him out. The people at the mouth of the den, who had listened with painful anxiety, hearing the growling of the wolf, and supposing their friend to be in the most imminent danger, drew him forth with such celerity that his shirt was stripped over his head, and his skin severely lacerated. After he had adjusted his clothes, and loaded his gun with nine buck-shot, holding a torch in one hand, and the musket in the other, he descended the second time. When he drew nearer than before, the wolf, assuming a still more fierce and terrible appearance, howling, rolling her eyes, snapping her teeth, and dropping her head between her legs, was evidently in the attitude, and on the point of springing at him. At the critical instant he levelled and fired at her head. Stunned with the shock, and suffocated with the smoke, he immediately found himself drawn out of the cave. But having refreshed himself, and permitted the smoke to dissipate, he went down the third time. Once more he came within sight of the wolf, who appearing very passive, he applied the torch to her nose; and perceiving her dead, he took hold of her ears, and then kicking the rope (still tied round his legs) the people above, with no small exultation, dragged them both out together.

I have offered these facts in greater detail, because they contain a display of character; and because they have been erroneously related in several European publications, and very much mutilated in the history of Connecticut, a work as replete with falsehood as destitute of genius, lately printed in London.

Prosperity, at length, began to attend the agricultural affairs of Mr. Putnam. He was acknowledged to be a skilful and indefatigable manager. His fields were mostly enclosed with stone walls. His crops commonly succeeded, because the land was well tilled and manured. His pastures and meadows became luxuriant. His cattle were of the best breed, and in good order. His garden and fruit-trees prolific. With the avails of the surplusage of his produce, foreign articles were purchased. Within doors he found the compensation of his labours in the plenty of excellent provisions, as well as in the happiness of domestic society.

A more particular description of his transition from narrow to easy circumstances might be given; but the mind that shall have acquired an idea of the habits of labour and simplicity, to which the industrious colonists were accustomed, will readily supply the omission. The effect of this gradual acquisition of property, generally favourable to individual virtue and public felicity, should not, however, be passed over in silence. If there is something fascinating in the charms of a country life, from the contemplation of beautiful landscapes, there is likewise something elevating to the soul, in the consciousness of being lord of the soil, and having the power of creating them. The man can scarcely be guilty of a sordid action, or even descend to an ungenerous thought, who, removed from the apprehension of want, sees his farm daily meliorating and assuming whatever appearance he pleases to prescribe. This situation converts the farmer into a species of rural philosopher, by inspiring an honest pride in his rank as a freeman, flattering the natural propensity for personal independence, and nourishing an unlimited hospitality and philanthropy in his social character.

But the time had now arrived which was to turn the instruments of husbandry into weapons of hostility, and to exchange the hunting of wolves, who had ravaged the sheep-folds, for the pursuit after savages, who had desolated the frontiers. Mr. Putnam was about thirty-seven years old when the war between England and France, which preceded the last, broke out in America. His reputation must have been favourably known to the government, since among the first troops that were levied by Connecticut in 1755, he was appointed to the command of a company in Lyman's regiment of Provincials. I have mentioned his age at this period expressly to obviate a prevalent opinion, that he was far advanced in life when he commenced his military service.

As he was extremely popular, he found no difficulty in enlisting his complement of recruits from the most hardy, enterprising, and respectable young men of his neighbourhood. The regiment joined the army, at the opening of the campaign, not far distant from Crown-Point. Soon after his arrival at camp, he became acquainted with the famous partizan Captain, afterwards Major Rogers, with whom he was frequently associated in traversing the wilderness, reconnoitering the enemy's lines, gaining intelligence, and taking straggling prisoners, as well as in beating up the quarters and surprising the advanced pickets of their army. For these operations, a corps of rangers were formed from the irregulars. The first time Rogers and Putnam were detached with a party of these light troops, it was the fortune of the latter to preserve, with his own hand, the life of the former, and to cement their friendship with the blood of one of their enemies.

The object of this expedition was to obtain an accurate knowledge of the position and state of the works at Crown-Point. It was impracticable to approach with their party near enough for this purpose, without being discovered. Alone, the undertaking was sufficiently hazardous, on account of the swarms of hostile Indians who infested the woods. Our two partizans, however, left all their men at a convenient distance, with strict orders to continue concealed until their return. Having thus cautiously taken their arrangements, they advanced with the profoundest silence in the evening; and lay, during the night, contiguous to the fortress. Early in the morning they approached so close as to be able to give satisfactory information to the General who had sent them, on the several points to which their attention had been directed: but Captain Rogers, being at a little distance from Captain Putnam, fortuitously met a stout Frenchman, who instantly seized his fuzee with one hand, and with the other attempted to stab him, while he called to an adjacent guard for assistance. The guard answered. Putnam, perceiving the imminent danger of his friend, and that no time was to be lost, or farther alarm given by firing, ran rapidly to them, while they were yet struggling, and with the butt-end of his piece, laid the Frenchman dead at his feet. The partizans, to elude pursuit, precipitated their flight, joined the party, and returned without loss to the encampment. Not many occasions occurred for partizans to display their talents in the course of this summer. The war was chequered with various fortune in different quarters— such as the total defeat of General Braddock, and the splendid victory of Sir William Johnson over the French troops, commanded by the Baron Dieskau. The brilliancy of this success was necessary to console the Americans for the disgrace of that disaster. Here I might, indeed, take a pride in contrasting the conduct of the British Regulars, who had been ambuscaded on the Monongahela, with that of the Provincials (under Johnson) who, having been attacked in their lines, gallantly repulsed the enemy, and took their General prisoner, did I consider myself at liberty to swell this essay with reflections on events, in which Putnam was not directly concerned. The time for which the colonial troops engaged to serve terminated with the campaign. Putnam was re-appointed, and again took the field in 1756.

Few are so ignorant of war as not to know, that military adventures in the night are always extremely liable to accidents. Captain Putnam having been commanded to reconnoitre the enemy's camp at *the Ovens,* near *Ticonderoga,* took the brave Lieutenant Robert Durkee as his companion. In attempting to execute these orders, he narrowly missed being taken himself in the first instance, and killing his friend in the second. It was customary for the British and Provincial troops to place their fires round their camp, which frequently exposed them to the enemy's scouts and patrols. A contrary practice, then unknown in the English army, prevailed among the French and Indians. The plan was much more rational; they kept their fires in the centre, lodged their men circularly at a distance, and posted their sentinels in the surrounding darkness. Our partizans approached the camp—and supposing the sentries were within the circle of fires, crept upon their hands and knees with the greatest possible caution, until, to their utter astonishment, they found themselves in the thickest of the enemy. The sentinels, discovering them, fired, and slightly wounded Durkee in the thigh. He and Putnam had no alternative. They fled. The latter being foremost, and scarcely able to see his hand before him, soon plunged into a clay-pit. Durkee, almost at the identical moment, came tumbling after. Putnam, by no means pleased at finding a companion, and believing him to be one of the enemy, lifted his tomahawk to give the deadly blow—when Durkee (who had followed so closely as to know him) inquired whether he had escaped unhurt. Captain Putnam, instantly recognizing the voice, dropped his weapon; and both, springing from the pit, made good their retreat to the neighbouring ledges, amidst a shower of random shot. There they betook themselves to a large log, by the side of which they lodged the remainder of the night. Before they lay down, Captain Putnam said he had a little rum in his canteen, which could never be more acceptable or necessary; but, on examining the canteen, which hung under his arm, he found the enemy had pierced it with their balls, and that there was not a drop of liquor left. The next day he found fourteen bullet holes in his blanket.

In the same summer, a body of the enemy, consisting of six hundred men, attacked the baggage and provision waggons at a place called the Half-Way-Brook; it being equi-distant from Fort Edward and the south end of Lake George. Having killed the oxen, and plundered the waggons, they retreated with their booty without having met with such resistance as might have been expected from the strength of the escort. General Webb, upon receiving intelligence of this disaster, ordered the Captains Putnam and Rogers

> to take one hundred volunteers in boats, with two wall-pieces, and two blunderbusses, and to proceed down Lake George to a certain point, there to leave the batteaux under a proper guard, and thence to cross by land, so as to harass, and, if practicable, intercept the retreating enemy at the Narrows.

These orders were executed with so much punctuality, that the party arrived at the destined place half an hour before the hostile boats came in view. Here they waited, under cover, until the enemy (ignorant of these proceedings) entered the Narrows, with their batteaux loaded with plunder. Then the volunteers poured upon them volley after volley, killed many of the oarsmen, sunk a number of the batteaux, and would soon have destroyed the whole body of the enemy, had not the unusual precipitancy of their passage (favoured by the wind) carried them through the Narrows into the wide part of South-Bay, where they were out of the reach of musket-shot. The shattered remnant of the little fleet soon arrived at Ticonderoga, and gave information that Putnam and Rogers were at the Narrows. A fresh party was instantly detached to cut them in pieces, on their return to Fort Edward. Our partizans, sensible of the probability of such an attempt, and being full twenty miles from their boats, strained every nerve to reach them as soon as possible; which they effected the same night. Next day, when they had returned as far as Sabbath-Day-Point, they discovered, on shore, the before-mentioned detachment of three hundred men, who had passed them in the night, and who now, on perceiving our party, took to their boats with the greatest alacrity, and rowed out to give battle. They advanced in line, maintaining a good mein, and felicitating themselves upon the prospect of an easy conquest, from the great superiority of their numbers. Flushed with these expectations, they were permitted to come within pistol-shot before a gun was fired. At once the wall-pieces and blunderbusses, which had been brought to rake them in the most vulnerable point, were discharged. As no such reception had been foreseen, the assailants were thrown into the utmost disorder. Their terror and confusion were greatly increased by a well-directed and most destructive fire of the small arms. The larger pieces being re-loaded, without annoyance, continued, alternately with the musketry, to make dreadful havock, until the rout was completed, and the enemy driven back to Ticonderoga. In this action, one of the bark canoes contained twenty Indians, of whom fifteen were killed. Great numbers, from other boats, both of French and Indians, were seen to fall overboard: but the account of their total loss could never be ascertained. Rogers and Putnam had but one man killed, and two slightly wounded. They now landed on the Point, and having refreshed their men at leisure, returned in good order to the British camp.

Soon after these rencounters, a singular kind of race was run by our nimble-footed Provincial and an active young Frenchman. The liberty of each was by turns at stake. General Webb, wanting a prisoner for the sake of intelligence, sent Captain Putnam, with five men, to procure one. The Captain concealed himself near the road which leads from Ticonderoga to the Ovens. His men seemed fond of showing themselves, which unsoldier-like conduct he prohibited with the severest reprehension. This rebuke they imputed to unnecessary fear. The observation is as true as vulgar, that persons distinguishable for temerity, when there is no apparent danger, are generally poltroons whenever danger approaches. They had not lain long in the high grass before a Frenchman and an Indian passed—the Indian was considerably in advance. As soon as the former had gone by, Putnam, relying on the fidelity of his men, sprang up, ran, and ordered them to follow. After running about thirty rods, he seized the Frenchman by the shoulders, and forced him to surrender: But his prisoner, looking round, perceiving no other enemy, and knowing the Indian would be ready in a moment to assist him, began to make an obstinate resistance. Putnam, finding himself betrayed by his men into a perilous dilemma, let go his hold, stepped back and snapped his piece, which was levelled at the Frenchman's breast. It missed fire. Upon this he thought it most prudent to retreat. The Frenchman, in turn, chased him back to his men, who, at last, raised themselves from the grass; which his pursuer espying in good time for himself, made his escape. Putnam, mortified that these men had frustrated his success, dismissed them with disgrace; and not long after accomplished his object. Such little feats as the capture of a single prisoner may be of infinitely more consequence than some, who are unacquainted with military affairs, would be apt to imagine. In a country covered with woods, like that part of America, then the seat of war, the difficulty of procuring, and the importance of possessing good intelligence, can scarcely be conceived even by European commanders. They, however, who know its value, will not appreciate lightly the services of an able partizan.

Nothing worthy of remark happened during this campaign, except the loss of Oswego. That fort, which had been built by General Shirley, to protect the peltry trade, cover the country on the Mohawk-River, and facilitate an invasion of Canada, by

Frontenac and Niagara, fell into the hands of the enemy, with a garrison of sixteen hundred men, and one hundred pieces of cannon.

The active services of Captain Putnam, on every occasion, attracted the admiration of the public, and induced the Legislature of Connecticut to promote him to a majority in 1757.

Lord Loudon was then Commander in Chief of the British forces in America. The expedition against Crown-Point, which, from the commencement of hostilities, had been in contemplation, seemed to give place to a more important operation that was meditated against Louisbourg. But the arrival of the Brest squadron at that place prevented the attempt; and the loss of Fort William Henry served to class this with the two former unsuccessful campaigns. It was rumoured, and partially credited at the time, that General Webb, who commanded in the northern department, had early intimation of the movement of the French army, and might have effectually succoured the garrison. The subsequent facts will place the affair in its proper light.

A few days before the siege, Major Putnam, with two hundred men, escorted General Webb from Fort Edward to Fort William Henry. The object was to examine the state of this fortification which stood at the southern extremity of Lake George. Several abortive attempts having been made by Major Rogers and others in the night season, Major Putnam proposed to go down the lake in open day-light, land at Northwest-Bay, and tarry on shore til he could make satisfactory discovery of the enemy's actual situation at Ticonderoga and the adjacent posts. The plan (which he suggested) of landing with only five men, and sending back the boats, to prevent detection, was deemed too hazardous by the General. At length, however, he was permitted to proceed with eighteen volunteers in three whale-boats; but before he arrived at Northwest-Bay, he discovered a body of men on an island. Immediately upon this he left two boats to fish at a distance, that they might not occasion an alarm, and returned himself with the information. The General, seeing him rowing back with great velocity, in a single boat, concluded the others were captured, and sent a skiff, with orders for him alone to come on shore. After advising the General of the circumstances, he urged the expediency of returning to make further discoveries, and bring off the boats. Leave was reluctantly given. He found his people, and, passing still onward, discovered (by the aid of a good perspective glass) a large army in motion. By this time several of the advanced canoes had nearly surrounded him, but by the swiftness of his whaleboats, he escaped through the midst of them. On his return, he informed the General minutely of all he had seen, and intimated his conviction that the expedition must obviously be destined against Fort William Henry. That Commander, strictly enjoining silence on the subject, directed him to put his men under an oath of secrecy, and to prepare, without loss of time, to return to the Head-Quarters of the army. Major Putnam observed, "he hoped his Excellency did not intend to neglect so fair an opportunity of giving battle, should the enemy presume to land." "What do you think we should do here?" replied the General. Accordingly, the next day he returned, and the day after Colonel Monro was ordered from Fort Edward, with his regiment, to reinforce the garrison. That officer took with him all his rich baggage and camp equipage, notwithstanding Major Putnam's advice to the contrary. The day following his arrival, the enemy landed and besieged the place.

The Marquis de Montcalm, Commander in Chief for the French in Canada (intending to take advantage of the absence of a large proportion of the British force, which he understood to be employed under Lord Loudon against Louisbourg) had assembled whatever men could be spared from Ticonderoga,

Crown-Point and the other garrisons: with these he had combined a considerable corps of Canadians, and a larger body of Indians than had ever before been collected; making, in the whole, an army of nearly eight thousand men. Our garrison consisted of twenty-five hundred, and was commanded by Colonel Monro, a very gallant officer, who found the means of sending express after express, to General Webb, with an account of his situation, and the most pressing solicitation for succour. In the mean time, the army at Fort Edward, which originally amounted to about four thousand, had been considerably augmented by Johnson's troops and the militia. On the eighth or ninth day after the landing of the French, General Johnson (in consequence of repeated applications) was suffered to march for the relief of the garrison, with all the Provincials, Militia, and Putnam's Rangers: but before they had proceeded three miles, the order was countermanded, and they returned. M. de Montcalm informed Major Putnam, when a prisoner in Canada, that one of his running Indians saw and reported this movement; and, upon being questioned relatively to the numbers, answered in their figurative stile, *"If you can count the leaves on the trees, you can count them."* In effect, the operations of the siege were suspended, and preparations made for re-embarking, when another of the runners reported that the detachment had gone back. The Marquis de Montcalm, provided with a good train of artillery, meeting with no annoyance from the British army, and but inconsiderable interruption from the garrison, accelerated his approaches so rapidly, as to obtain possession of the fort in a short time after completing the investiture. An intercepted letter from General Webb, advising the surrender, was sent into the fort to Colonel Monro by the French General.

The garrison engaged not to serve for eighteen months, and were permitted to march out with the honours of war. But the savages regarded not the capitulation, nor could they be restrained, by the utmost exertion of the commanding officer, from committing the most outrageous acts of cruelty. They stripped and plundered all the prisoners, and murdered great numbers in cold blood. Those who escaped by flight, or the protection of the French, arrived in a forlorn condition at Fort Edward: among these was the commandant of the garrison.

The day succeeding this deplorable scene of carnage and barbarity, Major Putnam having been dispatched with his Rangers to watch the motions of the enemy, came to the shore, when their rear was scarcely beyond the reach of musket-shot. They had carried off all the cannon, stores and water-craft. The fort was demolished. The barracks, the out-houses and suttlers' booths were heaps of ruins. The fires, not yet extinct, and the smoke, offensive from the mucilaginous nature of the fuel, but illy concealed innumerable fragments of human skulls and bones, and, in some instances, carcases half consumed. Dead bodies, weltering in blood, were every where to be seen, violated with all the wanton mutilations of savage ingenuity. More than one hundred women, some with their brains still oozing from the battered heads, others with their whole hair wrenched collectively with the skin from the bloody skulls, and many (with their throats cut) most inhumanly stabbed and butchered, lay stripped entirely naked, with their bowels torn out, and afforded a spectacle too horrible for description.

Not long after this misfortune, General Lyman succeeded to the command of Fort Edward. He resolved to strengthen it. For this purpose one hundred and fifty men were employed in cutting timber. To cover them, Captain Little was posted (with fifty British Regulars) at the head of a thick swamp, about one hundred rods eastward of the fort—to which his communication lay over a tongue of land, formed on the one side by the swamp, and by a creek on the other.

One morning at day-break, a sentinel saw indistinctly several birds, as he conceived, come from the swamp and fly over him with incredible swiftness. While he was ruminating on these wonderful birds, and endeavouring to form some idea of their colour, shape and size, an arrow buried itself in the limb of a tree just above his head. He now discovered the quality and design of these winged messengers of fate, and gave the alarm. Instantly the working party began to retreat along the defile. A large body of savages had concealed themselves in the morass before the guard was posted, and were attempting in this way to kill the sentinel without noise, with design to surprise the whole party. Finding the alarm given, they rushed from the covert, shot and tomahawked those who were nearest at hand, and pressed hard on the remainder of the unarmed fugitives. Captain Little flew to their relief, and, by pouring on the Indians a well-timed fire, checked the pursuit, and enabled such of the fatigue-men as did not fall in the first onset, to retire to the fort. Thither he sent for assistance, his little party being almost overpowered by numbers. But the commandant, imagining that the main body of the enemy were approaching for a general assault, called in his outposts and shut the gates.

Major Putnam lay with his Rangers on an island adjacent to the fort. Having heard the musketry, and learned that his friend Captain Little was in the utmost peril, he plunged into the river at the head of his corps, and waded through the water towards the place of engagement. This brought him so near to the fort, that General Lyman, apprized of his design, and unwilling that the lives of a few more brave men should be exposed to what he deemed inevitable destruction, mounted the parapet and ordered him to proceed no further. The Major only took time to make the best short apology he could, and marched on. This is the only instance in the whole course of his military service wherein he did not pay the strictest obedience to orders; and in this instance his motive was highly commendable. But when such conduct, even if sanctified by success, is passed over with impunity, it demonstrates that all is not right in the military system. In a disciplined army, such as that of the United States became under General Washington, an officer guilty of a slighter violation of orders, however elevated in rank or meritorious in service, would have been brought before the bar of a court-martial. Were it not for the seductive tendency of a brave man's example, I might have been spared the mortification of making these remarks on the conduct of an officer, whose distinguishing characteristics were promptitude for duty and love of subordination, as well as cheerfulness to encounter every species of difficulty and danger.

The Rangers of Putnam soon opened their way for a junction with the little handful of Regulars, who still obstinately maintained their ground. By his advice, the whole rushed impetuously with shouts and huzzas into the swamp. The savages fled on every side, and were chased, with no inconsiderable loss on their part, as long as the day-light lasted. On ours only one man was killed in the pursuit. His death was immediately revenged by that of the Indian who shot him. This Indian was one of the runners—a chosen body of active young men, who are made use of, not only to procure intelligence and convey tidings, but also to guard the rear on a retreat.

Here it will not be unseasonable to mention some of the customs in war peculiar to the aborigines, which, on the present as well as other occasions, they put in practice. Whenever a retreating, especially a flying party had gained the summit of a rising ground, they secreted one or two runners behind trees, copses, or bushes to fire at the enemy upon their ascending the hill. This commonly occasioned the enemy to halt and form for battle. In the interim, the runners used such dexterity as to be rarely discovered, or if discovered, they vanished behind the height and rejoined their brother-warriors, who having thus stolen a distance, were oftentimes seen by their pursuers no more. Or if the pursuers were too eager, they seldom failed to atone for their rashness by falling into an ambuscade. The Mohawks, who were afterwards much employed in scouts under the orders of Major Putnam, and who were perfectly versed in all the wiles and stratagems of their countrymen, showed him the mode of avoiding the evils of either alternative. In suspicious thickets, and at the borders of every considerable eminence, a momentary pause was made, while they, in different parts, penetrated or ascended with a cautiousness that cannot be easily described. They seemed all eye and ear. When they found no lurking mischief, they would beckon with the hand, and pronounce the word "OWISH," with a long labial hissing, the O being almost quiescent. This was ever the watch-word for the main body to advance.

Indians who went to war together, and who, for any reason found it necessary to separate into different routes, always left two or three runners at the place of separation, to give timely notice to either party in case of pursuit.

If a warrior chanced to straggle and lose himself in the woods, or be retarded by accident or wound, the party missing him would frequently, on their march, break down a bush or a shrub, and leave the top pointing in the direction they had gone, that the straggler, when he should behold it, might shape his course accordingly.

We come to the campaign when General Abercrombie took the command at Fort Edward. That General ordered Major Putnam, with sixty men, to proceed by land to South-Bay, on Lake George, for the purpose of making discoveries, and intercepting the enemy's parties. The latter, in compliance with these orders, posted himself at Wood-Creek, near its entrance into South-Bay. On this bank, which forms a jutting precipice ten or twelve feet above the water, he erected a stone parapet thirty feet in length, and masked it with young pine-trees, cut at a distance, and so artfully planted as to imitate the natural growth. From hence he sent back fifteen of his men, who had fallen sick. Distress for want of provisions, occasioned by the length of march, and time spent on this temporary fortification, compelled him to deviate from a rule he had established, never to permit a gun to be fired but at an enemy while on a scout. He was now obliged himself to shoot a buck, which had jumped into the Creek, in order to eke out their scanty subsistence until the fourth day after the completion of the works. About ten o'clock that evening, one of the men on duty at the margin of the bay, informed him that a fleet of bark canoes, filled with men, was steering towards the mouth of the Creek. He immediately called in all his sentinels, and ordered every man to his post. A profound stillness reigned in the atmosphere, and the full moon shone with uncommon brightness. The creek, which the enemy entered, is about six rods wide, and the bank opposite to the parapet above twenty feet high. It was intended to permit the canoes in front to pass—they had accordingly just passed, when a soldier accidentally struck his firelock against a stone. The commanding officer in the van canoe heard the noise, and repeated several times the savage watch-word, OWISH! Instantly the canoes huddled together, with their centre precisely in front of the works, covering the creek for a considerable distance above and below. The officers appeared to be in deep consultation, and the fleet on the point of returning, when Major Putnam, who had ordered his men in the most peremptory manner not to fire until he should set the example, gave the signal, by discharging his piece. They fired. Nothing could exceed the inextricable confusion and apparent consternation occasioned by this well-concerted attack. But, at last, the enemy finding, from the unfrequency (though there was no absolute intermission) in the firing, that the number of our men must be small, resolved to land below, and surround them. Putnam, apprehensive of this from the movement, sent Lieutenant Robert Durkee,* with twelve men, about thirty rods down the creek, who arrived in time to repulse the party which attempted to land. Another small detachment, under Lieutenant Parsons, was ordered up the creek to prevent any similar attempt. In the mean time Major Putnam kept up, through the whole night, an incessant and deadly fire on the main body of the enemy, without receiving any thing in return but shot void of effect, accompanied with dolorous groans, miserable shrieks, and dismal savage yells. After day-break he was advised that one part of the enemy had effected a landing considerably below, and were rapidly advancing to cut off his retreat. Apprised of the great superiority still opposed to him, as well as of the situation of his own soldiers, some of whom were entirely destitute of ammunition, and the rest reduced to one or two rounds per man, he commanded them to swing their packs. By hastening the retreat, in good order, they had just time to retire far enough up the creek to prevent being enclosed. During this long-continued action, in which the Americans had slain at least five times their

* As the name of the brave Durkee will occur no more in these sheets, I may be indulged in mentioning his melancholy fate. He survived this war, and was appointed a Captain in that war which terminated in the acknowledgment of our Independence. In 1778 he was wounded and taken prisoner by the savages at the battle of Wioming, on the Susquehannah. Having been condemned to be burnt, the Indians kept him in the flames with pitchforks, until he expired in the most excruciating torments.

own number, only one Provincial and one Indian were wounded on their side. These unfortunate men had been sent off for camp in the night, with two men to assist them, and directions to proceed by Wood-Creek as the safest, though not the shortest route. But having taken a nearer way, they were pursued and overtaken by the Indians, who, from the blood on the leaves and bushes, believed that they were on the trail of our whole party. The wounded, despairing of mercy, and unable to fly, insisted that the well soldiers should make their escape, which, on a moment's deliberation, they effected. The Provincial, whose thigh was broken by a ball, upon the approach of the savages, fired his piece, and killed three of them; after which he was quickly hacked in pieces. The Indian, however, was saved alive. This man Major Putnam saw afterwards in Canada, where he likewise learned that his enemy, in the rencounter at Wood-Creek, consisted of five hundred French and Indians, under the command of the celebrated partizan Molang, and that no party, since the war, had suffered so severely, as more than one-half of those who went out never returned.

Our brave little company, reduced to forty in number, had proceeded along the bank of the creek about an hour's march, when Major Putnam, being in front, was fired upon by a party just at hand. He, rightly appreciating the advantage often obtained by assuming a bold countenance on a critical occasion, in a stentorophonick tone, ordered his men to rush on the enemy, and promised that they should soon give a good account of them. It proved to be a scout of Provincials, who conceived they were firing upon the French; but the commanding officer, knowing Putnam's voice, cried out, "that they were all friends." Upon this the Major told him abruptly, "that, friends or enemies, they all deserved to be hanged for not killing more when they had so fair a shot." In fact, but one man was mortally wounded. While these things were transacted, a faithful soldier, whose ammunition had been early exhausted, made his way to the fort, and gave such information, that General Lyman was detached with five hundred men to cover the retreat. Major Putnam met them at only twelve miles distance from the fort, to which they returned the next day.

In the winter of 1757, when Colonel Haviland was Commandant at Fort Edward, the barracks adjoining to the north-west bastion took fire. They extended within twelve feet of the magazine, which contained three hundred barrels of powder. On its first discovery, the fire raged with great violence. The Commandant endeavoured, in vain, by discharging some pieces of heavy artillery against the supporters of this flight of barracks, to level them with the ground. Putnam arrived from the island where he was stationed at the moment when the blaze approached that end which was contiguous to the magazine. Instantly a vigorous attempt was made to extinguish the conflagration. A way was opened by a postern gate to the river, and the soldiers were employed in bringing water; which he, having mounted on a ladder to the eves of the building, received and threw upon the flame. It continued, notwithstanding their utmost efforts, to gain upon them. He stood, enveloped in smoke, so near the sheet of fire, that a pair of thick blanket mittens were burnt entirely from his hands; he was supplied with another pair dipt in water. Colonel Haviland, fearing that he would perish in the flames, called to him to come down. But he entreated that he might be suffered to remain, since destruction must inevitably ensue if their exertions should be remitted. The gallant Commandant, not less astonished than charmed at the boldness of his conduct, forbade any more effects to be carried out of the Fort, animated the men to redoubled diligence, and exclaimed, "if we must be blown up, we will go all together." At last when the barracks were seen to be tumbling, Putnam descended, placed himself at the interval, and continued from an incessant rotation of replenished buckets to pour water upon the magazine. The outside planks were already consumed by the proximity of the fire, and as only one thickness of timber intervened, the trepidation now became general and extreme. Putnam, still undaunted, covered with a cloud of cinders, and scorched with the intensity of the heat, maintained his position until the fire subsided, and the danger was wholly over. He had contended for one hour and a half with that terrible element. His legs, his thighs, his arms, and his face were blistered; and when he pulled off his second pair of mittens, the skin from his hands and fingers followed them. It was a month before he recovered. The Commandant, to whom his merits had before endeared him, could not stifle the emotions of gratitude, due to the man who had been so instrumental in preserving the magazine, the fort, and the garrison.

The repulse before Ticonderoga took place in 1758. General Abercrombie, the British Commander in Chief in America, conducted the expedition. His army, which amounted to nearly sixteen thousand Regulars and Provincials, was amply supplied with artillery and military stores. This well-appointed corps passed over Lake George, and landed, without opposition, at the point of destination. The troops advanced in columns. Lord Howe having Major Putnam with him, was in front of the centre. A body of about five hundred men, (the advance or pickets of the French army) which had fled at first, began to skirmish with our left. "Putnam," said Lord Howe, "what means that firing?" "I know not, but with your Lordship's leave will see," replied the former. "I will accompany you," rejoined the gallant young nobleman. In vain did Major Putnam attempt to dissuade him, by saying—"My Lord, if I am killed, the loss of my life will be of little consequence, but the preservation of yours is of infinite importance to this army." The only answer was, "Putnam, your life is as dear to you as mine is to me; I am determined to go." One hundred of the van, under Major Putnam, filed off with Lord Howe. They soon met the left flank of the enemy's advance, by whose first fire his Lordship fell. It was a loss indeed; and particularly felt in the operations which occurred three days afterwards. His manners and his virtues had made him the idol of the army. From his first arrival in America he had accommodated himself* and his regiment to the peculiar nature of the service. Exemplary to the office, a friend of the soldier, the model of discipline, he had not failed to encounter every hardship and hazard. Nothing could be more calculated to inspire men with the rash animation of rage, or to temper it with the cool perseverance of revenge, than the sight of such a hero, so beloved, fallen in his country's cause. It had the effect. Putnam's party, having cut their way obliquely through the enemy's ranks, and having been joined by Captain D'Ell, with twenty men, together with some other small parties, charged them so furiously in rear, that nearly three hundred were killed on the spot, and one hundred and forty-eight made prisoners. In the mean time, from the unskilfulness of the guides, some of our columns were bewildered. The left wing, seeing Putnam's party in their front, advancing over the dead bodies towards them, commenced a brisk and heavy fire, which killed a sergeant and several privates. Nor could they, by sounds or signs, be convinced of their mistake, until Major Putnam, preferring (if heaven had thus ordained it) the loss of his own life to the

---

* He cut his hair short, and induced the regiment to follow the example. He fashioned their cloathing for the activity of service, and divested himself and them of every article of superfluous baggage.

loss of the lives of his brave associates, ran through the midst of the flying balls, and prevented the impending catastrophe.

The tender feelings which Major Putnam possessed taught him to respect an unfortunate foe, and to strive, by every lenient art in his power, to alleviate the miseries of war. For this purpose he remained on the field until it began to grow dark, employed in collecting such of the enemy as were left wounded, to one place; he gave them all the liquor and little refreshments which he could procure; he furnished to each of them a blanket; he put three blankets under a French sergeant who was badly wounded through the body, and placed him in an easy posture by the side of a tree: the poor fellow could only squeeze his hand with an expressive grasp. "Ah," said Major Putnam, "depend upon it, my brave soldier, you shall be brought to the camp as soon as possible, and the same care shall be taken of you as if you were my brother." The next morning Major Rogers was sent to reconnoitre the field, and to bring off the wounded prisoners; but finding the wounded unable to help themselves, in order to save trouble, he dispatched every one of them to the world of spirits. Putnam's was not the only heart that bled. The Provincial and British officers who became acquainted with the fact, were struck with inexpressible horror.

Ticonderoga is surrounded on three sides by water; on the fourth, for some distance, extends a dangerous morass; the remainder was then fortified with a line eight feet high, and planted with artillery. For one hundred yards in front the plain was covered with great trees, cut for the purpose of defence, whose interwoven and sharpened branches projected outwards. Notwithstanding these impediments, the engineer who had been employed to reconnoitre, reported as his opinion, that the works might be carried with musketry. The difficulty and delay of dragging the battering cannon over grounds almost impracticable, induced the adoption of this fatal advice—to which, however, a rumour that the garrison, already consisting of four or five thousand men, was on the point of being augmented with three thousand more, probably contributed. The attack was as spirited in execution as ill-judged in design. The assailants, after having been for more than four hours exposed to a most fatal fire, without making any impression by their reiterated and obstinate proofs of valour, were ordered to retreat. Major Putnam, who had acted as an aid in bringing the Provincial regiments successively to action, assisted in preserving order. It was said that a great number of the enemy were shot in the head, every other part having been concealed behind their works. The loss on our side was upwards of two thousand killed and wounded. Twenty-five hundred stands of arms were taken by the French. Our army, after sustaining this havock, retreated with such extraordinary precipitation, that they regained their camp at the southward of Lake George the evening after the action.

The successes in other parts of America made amends for this defeat. Louisbourg, after a vigorous siege, was reduced by the Generals Amherst and Wolfe: Frontenac, a post of importance on the communication between Lake Ontario and the St. Lawrence, surrendered to Colonel Bradstreet: and Fort Du-Quesne, situated at the confluence of Monongahela with the Ohio, (the possession of which had kindled the flame of war that now spread through the four quarters of the globe) was captured by General Forbes.

A few adventures, in which the public interests were little concerned, but which, from their peculiarity, appear worthy of being preserved, happened before the conclusion of the year. As one day Major Putnam chanced to lie with a batteau and five men, on the eastern shore of the Hudson, near the Rapids, contiguous to which Fort Miller stood, his men on the opposite bank had given him to understand, that a large body of savages were in his rear, and would be upon him in a moment. To stay and be sacrificed—to attempt crossing and be shot—or to go down to the falls, with an almost absolute certainty of being drowned, were the sole alternatives that presented themselves to his choice. So instantaneously was the latter adopted, that one man who had rambled a little from the party, was, of necessity, left, and fell a miserable victim to savage barbarity. The Indians arrived on the shore soon enough to fire many balls on the batteau before it could be got under way. No sooner had our batteau-men escaped, by favour of the rapidity of the current, beyond the reach of musket shot, than death seemed only to have been avoided in one form to be encountered in another not less terrible. Prominent rocks, latent shelves, absorbing eddies, and abrupt descents, for a quarter of a mile, afforded scarcely the smallest chance of escaping without a miracle. Putnam, trusting himself to a good Providence, whose kindness he had often experienced, rather than to men, whose tenderest mercies are cruelty, was now seen to place himself sedately at the helm, and afford an astonishing spectacle of serenity. His companions, with a mixture of terror, admiration and wonder, saw him incessantly changing the course, to avoid the jaws of ruin, that seemed expanded to swallow the whirling boat. Twice he turned it fairly round to shun the rifts of rocks. Amidst these eddies, in which there was the greatest danger of its foundering, at one moment the sides were exposed to the fury of the waves; then the stern, and next the bow glanced obliquely onward, with inconceivable velocity. With not less amazement the savages beheld him sometimes mounting the billows, then plunging abruptly down, at other times skilfully veering from the rocks, and shooting through the only narrow passage; until, at last, they viewed the boat safely gliding on the smooth surface of the stream below. At this sight, it is asserted, that these rude sons of nature were affected with the same kind of superstitious veneration which the Europeans, in the dark ages, entertained for some of their most valorous champions. They deemed the man invulnerable, whom their balls, on his pushing from shore, could not touch; and whom they had seen steering in safety down the rapids that had never before been passed. They conceived it would be an affront against the *Great Spirit* to attempt to kill this favoured mortal with powder and ball, if they should ever see and know him again.

In the month of August five hundred men were employed, under the orders of Majors Rogers and Putnam, to watch the motions of the enemy near Ticonderoga. At South-Bay they separated the party into two equal divisions, and Rogers took a position on Wood-Creek, twelve miles distant from Putnam.

Upon being, some time afterwards, discovered, they formed a re-union, and concerted measures for returning to Fort Edward. Their march through the woods was *in three divisions, by* FILES: the right commanded by Rogers, the left by Putnam, and the centre by Captain D'Ell. The first night they encamped on the banks of *Clear River*, about a mile from old Fort Ann, which had been formerly built by General Nicholson. Next morning Major Rogers, and a British officer, named Irwin, incautiously suffered themselves, from a spirit of false emulation, to be engaged in firing at a mark. Nothing could have been more repugnant to the military principles of Putnam than such conduct, or reprobated by him in more pointed terms. As soon as the heavy dew which had fallen the preceding night would permit, the detachment moved in one body, Putnam being in front, D'Ell in centre, and Rogers the rear. The impervious growth of shrubs and under-brush that had sprung up, where the land had been partially cleared some years before, occasioned this change in the order of march. At the moment of moving, the famous French partizan Molang, who had been sent with five hundred men to intercept our party, was not more than one mile and an half distant from them. Having heard the firing, he hasted to lay an ambuscade precisely in that part of the wood most favourable to his project. Major Putnam was just emerging from the thicket, into the common forest, when the enemy rose, and with discordant yells and whoops, commenced an attack upon the right of his division. Surprized, but undismayed, Putnam halted, returned the fire, and passed the word for the other divisions to advance for his support. D'Ell came. The action, though widely scattered, and principally fought between man and man, soon grew general and intensely warm. It would be as difficult as useless to describe this irregular and ferocious mode of fighting. Rogers came not up; but, as he declared afterwards, formed a circular file between our party and Wood-Creek, to prevent their being taken in rear or enfiladed. Successful as he commonly was, his conduct did not always pass without unfavourable imputation. Notwithstanding, it was a current saying in the camp, "that Rogers always *sent*, but Putnam *led* his men to action," yet, in justice, it ought to be remarked here, that the latter has never been known, in relating the story of this day's disaster, to affix any stigma upon the conduct of the former.

Major Putnam, perceiving it would be impracticable to cross the creek, determined to maintain his ground. Inspired by his example, the officers and men behaved with great bravery: sometimes they fought aggregately in open view, and sometimes individually under cover; taking aim from behind the bodies of trees, and acting in a manner independent of each other. For himself, having discharged his fuzee several times, at length it missed fire, while the muzzle was pressed against the breast of a large and well-proportioned savage. This *warrior,* availing himself of the indefensible attitude of his adversary, with a tremendous war-whoop, sprang forward, with his lifted hatchet, and compelled him to surrender; and having disarmed and bound him fast to a tree, returned to the battle.

The intrepid Captains D'Ell and Harman, who now commanded, were forced to give ground for a little distance: the savages, conceiving this to be the certain harbinger of victory, rushed impetuously on, with dreadful and redoubled cries. But our two partizans, collecting a handful of brave men, gave the pursuers so warm a reception as to oblige them, in turn, to retreat a little beyond the spot at which the action had commenced. Here they made a stand. This change of ground occasioned the tree to which Putnam was tied to be directly between the fire of the two parties. Human imagination can hardly figure to itself a more deplorable situation. The balls flew incessantly from either side, many struck the tree while some passed through the sleeves and skirts of his coat. In this state of jeopardy, unable to move his body, to stir his limbs, or even to incline his head, he remained more than an hour. So equally balanced, and so obstinate was the fight! At one moment, while the battle swerved in favour of the enemy, a young savage chose an odd way of discovering his humour. He found Putnam bound. He might have dispatched him at a blow. But he loved better to excite the terrors of the prisoner, by hurling a tomahawk at his head, or rather it should seem his object was to see how near he could throw it without touching him — the weapon struck in the tree a number of times at a hair's breadth distance from the mark. When the Indian had finished his amusement, a French bas-officer (a much more inveterate savage by nature, though descended from so humane and polished a nation) perceiving Putnam, came up to him, and, levelling a fuzee within a foot of his breast, attempted to discharge it—it missed fire. Ineffectually did the intended victim solicit the treatment due to his situation, by repeating that he was a prisoner of war. The degenerate Frenchman did not understand the language of honour or of nature: deaf to their voice, and dead to sensibility, he violently, and repeatedly, pushed the muzzle of his gun against Putnam's ribs, and finally, gave him a cruel blow on the jaw with the butt of his piece. After this dastardly deed he left him.

At length the active intrepidity of D'Ell and Harmon,* seconded by the persevering valour of their followers, prevailed. They drove from the field the enemy, who left about ninety dead behind them. As they were retiring, Putnam was untied by the Indian who had made him prisoner, and whom he afterwards called master. Having been conducted for some distance from the place of action, he was stripped of his coat, vest, stockings and shoes; loaded with as many of the packs of the wounded as could be piled upon him; strongly pinioned, and his wrists tied as closely together as they could be pulled with a cord. After he had marched, through no pleasant paths, in this painful manner, for many a tedious mile, the party (who were excessively fatigued) halted to breathe. His hands were now immoderately swelled from the tightness of the ligature; and the pain had become intolerable. His feet were so much scratched, that the blood dropped fast from them. Exhausted with bearing a burden above his strength, and frantic with torments exquisite beyond endurance, he entreated the Irish interpreter to implore, as the last and only grace he desired of the savages, that they

---

* This worthy officer is still living at Marlborough, in the State of Massachusetts.

would knock him on the head and take his scalp at once, or loose his hands. A French officer, instantly interposing, ordered his hands to be unbound, and some of the packs to be taken off. By this time the Indian who captured him, and had been absent with the wounded, coming up, gave him a pair of mocasons, and expressed great indignation at the unworthy treatment his prisoner had suffered.

That savage chief again returned to the care of the wounded, and the Indians, about two hundred in number, went before the rest of the party to the place where the whole were that night to encamp. They took with them Major Putnam, on whom, besides innumerable other outrages, they had the barbarity to inflict a deep wound with a tomahawk in the left cheek. His sufferings were in this place to be consummated. A scene of horror, infinitely greater than had ever met his eyes before, was now preparing. It was determined to roast him alive. For this purpose they led him into a dark forest, stripped him naked, bound him to a tree, and piled dry brush, with other fuel, at a small distance, in a circle round him. They accompanied their labours, as if for his funeral dirge, with screams and sounds inimitable but by savage voices. Then they set the piles on fire. A sudden shower damped the rising flame. Still they strove to kindle it, until, at last, the blaze ran fiercely round the circle. Major Putnam soon began to feel the scorching heat. His hands were so tied that he could move his body. He often shifted sides as the fire approached. This sight, at the very idea of which all but savages must shudder, afforded the highest diversion to his inhuman tormentors, who demonstrated the delirium of their joy by correspondent yells, dances, and gesticulations. He saw clearly that his final hour was inevitably come. He summoned all his resolution, and composed his mind, as far as the circumstances could admit, to bid an eternal farewell to all he held most dear.

To quit the world would scarcely have cost a single pang; but for the idea of home, but for the remembrance of domestic endearments, of the affectionate partner of his soul, and of their beloved offspring. His thought was ultimately fixed on a happier state of existence, beyond the tortures he was beginning to endure. The bitterness of death, even of that death which is accompanied with the keenest agonies, was, in a manner, past—nature, with a feeble struggle, was quitting its last hold on sublunary things—when a French officer rushed through the crowd, opened a way by scattering the burning brands, and unbound the victim. It was Molang himself—to whom a savage, unwilling to see another human sacrifice immolated, had run and communicated the tidings. That commandant spurned and severely reprimanded the barbarians, whose nocturnal powwas and hellish orgies he suddenly ended. Putnam did not want for feeling or gratitude. The French commander, fearing to trust him alone with them, remained until he could deliver him in safety into the hands of his master.

The savage approached his prisoner kindly, and seemed to treat him with particular affection. He offered him some hard biscuit; but finding that he could not chew them, on account of the blow he had received from the Frenchman, this more humane savage soaked some of the biscuit in water, and made him suck the pulp-like part. Determined, however, not to loose his captive (the refreshment being finished) he took the mocasons from his feet, and tied them to one of his wrists: then directing him to lie down on his back upon the bare ground, he stretched one arm to its full length, and bound it fast to a young tree; the other arm was extended and bound in the same manner—his legs were stretched apart and fastened to two saplings. Then a number of tall, but slender poles were cut down, which, with some long bushes, were laid across his body from head to foot:

on each side lay as many Indians as could conveniently find lodging, in order to prevent the possibility of his escape. In this disagreeable and painful posture he remained until morning. During this night, the longest and most dreary conceivable, our hero used to relate that he felt a ray of cheerfulness come casually across his mind, and could not even refrain from smiling when he reflected on this ludicrous group for a painter, of which he himself was the principal figure.

The next day he was allowed his blanket and mocasons, and permitted to march without carrying any pack, or receiving any insult. To allay his extreme hunger, a little bear's meat was given, which he sucked through his teeth. At night the party arrived at Ticonderoga, and the prisoner was placed under the care of a French guard. The savages, who had been prevented from glutting their diabolical thirst for blood, took other opportunity of manifesting their malevolence for the disappointment, by horrid grimaces and angry gestures; but they were suffered no more to offer violence or personal indignity to him.

After having been examined by the Marquis de Montcalm, Major Putnam was conducted to Montreal by a French officer, who treated him with the greatest indulgence and humanity.

At this place were several prisoners. Colonel Peter Schuyler, remarkable for his philanthropy, generosity, and friendship, was of the number. No sooner had he heard of Major Putnam's arrival, than he went to the interpreter's quarters, and inquired whether he had a Provincial Major in his custody? He found Major Putnam in a comfortless condition—without coat, waistcoat, or hose—the remnant of his cloathing miserably dirty and ragged—his beard long and squalid—his legs torn by thorns and briars—his face gashed with wounds and swolen with bruises. Colonel Schuyler, irritated beyond all sufferance at such a sight, could scarcely restrain his speech within limits, consistent with the prudence of a prisoner and the meekness of a christian. Major Putnam was immediately treated according to his rank, cloathed in a decent manner, and supplied with money by that liberal and sympathetic patron of the distressed.

The capture of Frontenac by General Bradstreet afforded occasion for an exchange of prisoners. Colonel Schuyler was comprehended in the cartel. A generous spirit can never be satisfied with imposing tasks for its generosity to accomplish. Apprehensive if it should be known that Putnam was a distinguished partizan, his liberation might be retarded, and knowing that there were officers who, from the length of their captivity, had a claim of priority to exchange, he had, by his happy address, induced the Governor to offer, that whatever officer he might think proper to nominate should be included in the present cartel. With great politeness in manner, but seeming indifference as to object, he expressed his warmest acknowledgments to the Governor, and said,

> There is an old man here, who is a Provincial Major, and wishes to be at home with his wife and children; he can do no good here or any where else: I believe your Excellency had better keep some of the young men, who have no wife or children to care for, and let the old fellow go home with me.

This justifiable finesse had the desired effect.

At the house of Colonel Schuyler, Major Putnam became acquainted with Mrs. Howe, a fair captive, whose history would not be read without emotion, if it could be written in the same affecting manner in which I have often heard it told. She was still young and handsome herself, though she had two daughters of marriageable age. Distress, which had taken somewhat from the original redundancy of her bloom, and added a softening paleness to her cheeks, rendered her appearance the more engaging. Her face, that seemed to have been formed for the assemblage of dimples and smiles, was clouded with care. The natural sweetness was not, however, soured by despondency and petulance, but chastened by humility and resignation. This mild daughter of sorrow looked as if she had known the day of prosperity, when serenity and gladness of soul were the inmates of her bosom. That day was past, and the once lively features now assumed a tender melancholy, which witnessed her irreparable loss. She needed not the customary weeds of mourning, or the fallacious pageantry of woe, to prove her widowed state. She was in that state of affliction when the excess is so far abated as to permit the subject to be drawn into conversation, without opening the wound afresh. It is then rather a source of pleasure than pain to dwell upon the circumstances in narration. Every thing conspired to make her story interesting. Her first husband had been killed and scalped by the Indians some years before. By an unexpected assault, in 1756, upon Fort Dummer, where she then happened to be present with Mr. Howe, her second husband, the savages carried the fort, murdered the greater part of the garrison, mangled in death her husband, and led her away with seven children into captivity. She was for some months kept with them; and during their rambles she was frequently on the point of perishing with hunger, and as often subjected to hardships seemingly intolerable to one of so delicate a frame. Some time after the career of her miseries began, the Indians selected a couple of their young men to marry her daughters. The fright and disgust which the intelligence of this intention occasioned to these poor young creatures, added infinitely to the sorrows and perplexities of their frantic mother. To prevent the hated connection, all the activity of female resource was called into exertion. She found an opportunity of conveying to the Governor a petition, that her daughters might be received into a convent for the sake of securing the salvation of their souls. Happily the pious fraud succeeded.

About the same time the savages separated, and carried off her other five children into different tribes. She was ransomed by an elderly French officer for four hundred livres. Of no avail were the cries of this tender mother—a mother desolated by the loss of her children, who were thus torn from her fond embraces, and removed many hundred miles from each other, into the utmost recesses of Canada. With them (could they have been kept together) she would most willingly have wandered to the extremities of the world, and accepted as a desirable portion the cruel lot of slavery for life. But she was precluded from the sweet hope of ever beholding them again. The insufferable pang of parting, and the idea of eternal separation, planted the arrows of despair deep in her soul. Though all the world was no better than a desert, and all its inhabitants were then indifferent to her, yet the loveliness of her appearance in sorrow had awakened affections, which, in the aggravation of her troubles, were to become a new source of afflictions.

The officer who bought her of the Indians had a son who also held a commission, and resided with his father. During her continuance in the same house, at St. John's, the double attachment of the father and the son rendered her situation extremely distressing. It is true, the calmness of age delighted to gaze respectfully on her beauty; but the impetuosity of youth was fired to madness by the sight of her charms. One day, the son, whose attentions had been long lavished upon her in vain, finding her alone in a chamber, forcibly seized her hand, and solemnly declared that he would now satiate the passion which she had so long refused to indulge. She recurred to entreaties, struggles, and tears, those prevalent female weapons which the distraction of danger not less than the promptness of genius is wont to supply; while he, in the delirium of vexation and desire, snatched a dagger, and swore he would put an end to her life if she persisted to struggle. Mrs. Howe, assuming the dignity of conscious virtue, told him it was what she most ardently wished, and begged him to plunge the poignard through her heart, since the mutual importunities and jealousies of such rivals had rendered her life, though innocent, more irksome and insupportable than death itself. Struck with a momentary compunction, he seemed to relent, and relax his hold; and she, availing herself of his irresolution, or absence of mind, escaped down the stairs. In her disordered state she told the whole transaction to his father, who directed her, in future, to sleep in a small bed at the foot of that in which his wife lodged. The affair soon reached the Governor's ears, and the young officer was, shortly afterwards, sent on a tour of duty to *Detroit*.

This gave her a short respite; but she dreaded his return, and the humiliating insults for which she might be reserved. Her children, too, were ever present to her melancholy mind. A stranger, a widow, a captive, she knew not where to apply for relief. She had heard of the name of Schuyler—she was yet to learn, that it was only another appellation for the friend of suffering humanity. As that excellent man was on his way from Quebec to the Jerseys, under a parole, for a limited time, she came, with feeble and trembling steps, to him. The same maternal passion which sometimes overcomes the timidity of nature in the birds, when plundered of their callow nestlings, emboldened her, notwithstanding her native diffidence, to disclose those griefs which were ready to devour her in silence. While her delicate aspect was heightened to a glowing blush, for fear of offending by an inexcusable importunity, or of transgressing the rules of propriety, by representing herself as being an object of admiration, she told, with artless simplicity, all the story of her woes. Colonel Schuyler, from that moment, became her protector, and endeavoured to procure her liberty. The person who purchased her from the savages, unwilling to part with so fair a purchase, demanded a thousand livres as her ransom. But Colonel Schuyler, on his return to Quebec, obtained from the Governor an order, in consequence of which Mrs. Howe was given up to him for four hundred livres; nor did his active goodness rest until every one of her five sons was restored to her.

Business having made it necessary that Colonel Schuyler should precede the prisoners who were exchanged, he recommended the fair captive to the protection of his friend Putnam. She had recovered from the meazles when the party was preparing to set off for New-England. By this time the young French officer had returned, with his passion rather increased than abated by absence. He pursued her wheresoever she went, and, although he could make no advances in her affection, he seemed resolved, by perseverance, to carry his point. Mrs. Howe, terrified by his treatment, was obliged to keep constantly near Major Putnam, who informed the young officer that he should protect that lady at the risk of his life.*

In the long march from captivity, through an inhospitable wilderness, encumbered with five small children, she suffered incredible hardships. Though endowed with masculine fortitude, she was truly feminine in strength, and must have fainted by the way, had it not been for the assistance of Major Putnam. Then were a thousand good offices which the helplessness of her condition demanded, and which the gentleness of his na-

* Two or three incidents respecting Mrs. Howe, which were received by the author from General Putnam, and inserted in the former editions, are omitted in this, as they appeared, on farther information, to be mistakes.

ture delighted to perform. He assisted in leading her little ones, and in carrying them over the swampy grounds and runs of water, with which their course was frequently intersected. He mingled his own mess with that of the widow and the fatherless, and assisted them in supplying and preparing their provisions. Upon arriving within the settlements, they experienced a reciprocal regret at separation, and were only consoled by the expectation of soon mingling in the embraces of their former acquaintances and dearest connections.

After the conquest of Canada, in 1760, she made a journey to Quebec, in order to bring back her two daughters, whom she had left in a convent. She found one of them married to a French officer. The other having contracted a great fondness for the religious sisterhood, with reluctance consented to leave them and return.

We now arrive at the period when the prowess of Britain, victorious alike by sea and by land, in the new and in the old world, had elevated that name to the zenith of national glory. The conquest of Quebec opened the way for the total reduction of Canada. On the side of the Lakes, Amherst having captured the posts of Ticonderoga and Crown-Point, applied himself to strengthen the latter. Putnam, who had been raised to the rank of Lieutenant-Colonel, and present at these operations, was employed the remainder of this and some part of the succeeding season, in superintending the parties which were detached to procure timber and other materials for the fortification.

In 1760, General Amherst, a sagacious, humane, and experienced commander, planned the termination of the war in Canada by a bloodless conquest. For this purpose, three armies were destined to co-operate, by different routes, against Montreal, the only remaining place of strength the enemy held in that country. The corps formerly commanded by General Wolfe, now by General Murray, was ordered to ascend the river St. Lawrence; another, under Colonel Haviland, to penetrate by the Isle Aux Noix; and the third, consisting of about ten thousand men, commanded by the General himself, after passing up the Mohawk-River, and taking its course by the Lake Ontario, was to form a junction by falling down the St. Lawrence. In this progress, more than one occasion presented itself to manifest the intrepidity and soldiership of Lieutenant-Colonel Putnam. Two armed vessels obstructed the passage, and prevented the attack on Oswegatchie. Putnam, with one thousand men, in fifty batteaux, undertook to board them. This dauntless officer, ever sparing of the blood of others, as prodigal of his own, to accomplish it with the less loss, put himself (with a chosen crew, a beetle and wedges) in the van, with a design to wedge the rudders, so that the vessels should not be able to turn their broadsides, or perform any other manoeuvre. All the men in his little fleet were ordered to strip to their waistcoats, and advance at the same time. He promised, if he lived, to join and show them the way up the sides. Animated by so daring an example, they moved swiftly, in profound stillness, as to certain victory or death. The people on both the ships, beholding the good countenance with which they approached, ran one of the vessels on shore, and struck the colours of the other. Had it not been for the dastardly conduct of the ship's company in the latter, who compelled the Captain to haul down his ensign, he would have given the assailants a bloody reception: for the vessels were well provided with spars, nettings, and every customary instrument of annoyance as well as defence.

It now remained to attack the fortress, which stood on an island, and seemed to have been rendered inaccessible by an high abattis of black-ash, that every where projected over the water. Lieutenant-Colonel Putnam proposed a mode of attack, and offered his services to carry it into effect. The General approved the proposal. Our partizan, accordingly, caused a sufficient number of boats to be fitted for the enterprize. The sides of each boat were surrounded with fascines, musket proof, which covered the men completely. A wide plank, twenty feet in length, was then fitted to every boat in such manner, by having an angular piece sawed from one extremity, that, when fastened by ropes on both sides of the bow, it might be raised or lowered at pleasure. The design was, that the plank should be held erect, while the oarsmen forced the bow with the utmost exertion against the abatis; and afterwards being dropped on the pointed brush, it should serve as a kind of bridge to assist the men in passing over them. Lieutenant-Colonel Putnam having made his dispositions to attempt the escalade in many places at the same moment, advanced with his boats in admirable order. The garrison perceiving these extraordinary and unexpected machines, waited not the assault, but capitulated. Lieutenant-Colonel Putnam was particularly honoured by General Amherst, for his ingenuity in this invention, and promptitude in its execution. The three armies arrived at Montreal within two days of each other; and the conquest of Canada became complete without the loss of a single drop of blood.

At no great distance from Montreal stands the savage village called Cochnawaga. Here our partizan found the Indian chief who had formerly made him prisoner. That Indian was highly delighted to see his old acquaintance, whom he entertained in his own well-built stone house with great friendship and hospitality; while his guest did not discover less satisfaction in an opportunity of shaking the brave savage by the hand, and proffering him protection in this reverse of his military fortunes.

When the belligerent powers were considerably exhausted, a rupture took place between Great-Britain and Spain, in the month of January, 1762, and an expedition was formed that campaign, under Lord Albemarle, against the Havannah. A body of Provincials, composed of five hundred men from the Jerseys, eight hundred from New-York, and one thousand from Connecticut, joined his Lordship. General Lyman, who raised the regiment of one thousand men in Connecticut, being the senior officer, commanded the whole: of course, the immediate command of his regiment devolved upon Lieutenant-Colonel Putnam. The fleet that carried these troops sailed from New-York, and arrived safely on the coast of Cuba. There a terrible storm arose, and the transport in which Lieutenant-Colonel Putnam had embarked with five hundred men, was wrecked on a rift of craggy rocks. The weather was so tempestuous, and the surf, which ran mountain-high, dashed with such violence against the ship, that the most experienced seamen expected it would soon part asunder. The rest of the fleet, so far from being able to afford assistance, with difficulty rode out the gale. In this deplorable situation, as the only expedient by which they could be saved, strict order was maintained, and all those people who best understood the use of tools, instantly employed in constructing rafts from spars, plank, and whatever other materials could be procured. There happened to be on board a large quantity of strong cords, (the same that are used in the whale fishery) which, being fastened to the rafts, after the first had with inconceivable hazard reached the shore, were of infinite service in preventing the others from driving out to sea, as also in dragging them athwart the billows to the beach; by which means every man was finally saved. With the same presence of mind to take advantage of circumstances, the same precaution to prevent confusion on similar occasions, how many valuable lives, prematurely lost, might have been preserved as blessings to their families, their friends, and their country! As soon as all were landed, Lieutenant-Colonel Putnam fortified his camp, that he might not be exposed to insult from the inhabitants of the neighbouring districts, or from those of Carthagena, who were but twenty-four miles distant. Here the party remained unmolested several days, until the storm had so much abated as to permit the convoy to take them off. They soon joined the troops before the Havannah, who, having been several weeks in that unhealthy climate, already began to grow extremely sickly.* The opportune arrival of the Provincial reinforcement, in perfect health, contributed not a little to forward the works, and hasten the reduction of that important place. But the Provincials suffered so miserably by sickness afterwards that very few ever returned to their native land again.

Although a general peace among the European powers was ratified in 1763, yet the savages on our western frontiers still continued their hostilities. After they had taken several posts, General Bradstreet was sent in 1764, with an army, against them. Colonel Putnam, then, for the first time, appointed to the command of a regiment, was on the expedition, as was the Indian chief whom I have several times had occasion to mention as his capturer, at the head of one hundred Cochnawaga warriors. Before General Bradstreet reached Detroit, which the savages invested, Captain D'Ell, the faithful friend and intrepid fellow soldier of Colonel Putnam, had been slain in a desperate

---

* Colonel Haviland, an accomplished officer, several times mentioned in these memoirs, who brought to America a regiment of one thousand Irish veterans, had but seventy men remaining alive when he left the Havannah. Colonel Haviland, during this siege, having once with his regiment engaged and routed five hundred Spaniards, met Colonel Putnam on his return, and said— "Putnam, give me a pinch of snuff." "I never carry any," returned Putnam. "I have always just such luck," cried Haviland; "the rascally Spaniards have shot away my pocket, snuffbox, and all."

sally. He having been detached with five hundred men, in 1763, by General Amherst, to raise the siege, found means of throwing the succour into the fort. But the garrison, commanded by Major Gladwine, a brave and sensible officer, had been so much weakened, by the lurking and insidious mode of war practised by the savages, that not a man could be spared to co-operate in an attack upon them. The Commandant would even have dissuaded Captain D'Ell from the attempt, on account of the great disparity in numbers; but the latter, relying on the discipline and courage of his men, replied, "God forbid that I should ever disobey the orders of my General," and immediately disposed them for action. It was obstinate and bloody; but the vastly superior number of the savages enabled them to enclose Captain D'Ell's party on every side, and compelled him, finally, to fight his way, in retreat from one stone-house to another. Having halted to breathe a moment, he saw one of his bravest sergeants lying at a small distance, wounded through the thigh, and wallowing in his blood. Whereupon he desired some of the men to run and bring the sergeant to the house, but they declined it. Then declaring, "that he never would leave so brave a soldier in the field to be tortured by the savages," he ran and endeavoured to help him up—at the instant a volley of shot dropped them both dead together. The party continued retreating from house to house until they regained the fort; where it was found the conflict had been so sharp, and lasted so long, that only fifty men remained alive of the five hundred who had sallied.

Upon the arrival of General Bradstreet, the savages saw that all further efforts, in arms, would be vain, and accordingly, after many fallacious proposals for a peace, and frequent tergiversations in the negotiation, they concluded a treaty, which ended the war in America.

Colonel Putnam, at the expiration of ten years from his first receiving a commission, after having seen as much service, endured as many hardships, encountered as many dangers, and acquired as many laurels as any officer of his rank, with great satisfaction laid aside his uniform, and returned to his plough. The various and uncommon scenes of war in which he had acted a respectable part, his intercourse with the world, and intimacy with some of the first characters in the army, joined with occasional reading, had not only brought into view whatever talents he possessed from nature, but, at the same time, had extended his knowledge, and polished his manners, to a considerable degree. Not having become inflated with pride, or forgetful of his old connections, he had the good fortune to possess entirely the good will of his fellow citizens. No character stood fairer in the public eye for integrity, bravery, and patriotism. He was employed in several offices in his own town, and not unfrequently elected to represent it in the General Assembly. The year after his return to private life, the minds of men were strangely agitated, by an attempt of the British Parliament to introduce the memorable Stamp Act in America. This germe policy, whose growth was repressed by the moderate temperature in which it was kept by some administrations, did not fully disclose its fruit until nearly eleven years afterwards. All the world knows how it then ripened into a civil war.

On the twenty-second day of March, 1765, the Stamp Act received the royal assent. It was to take place in America on the first day of November following. This innovation spread a sudden and universal alarm. The political pulse in the Provinces, from *Main* to *Georgia,* throbbed in sympathy. The Assemblies, in most of these colonies, that they might oppose it legally and in concert, appointed Delegates to confer together on the sub-

59

ject. This first Congress met, early in October, at New-York. They agreed upon a Declaration of Rights and Grievances of the Colonists; together with separate Addresses to the King, Lords, and Commons of Great-Britain. In the mean time, the people had determined, in order to prevent the stamped paper from being distributed, that the Stamp-Masters should not enter on the execution of their office. That appointment, in Connecticut, had been conferred upon Mr. Ingersol, a very dignified, sensible, and learned native of the colony, who, upon being solicited to resign, did not, in the first instance, give a satisfactory answer. In consequence of which, a great number of the substantial yeomanry, on horseback, furnished with provisions for themselves, and provender for their horses, assembled in the eastern counties, and began their march for New-Haven, to receive the resignation of Mr. Ingersol. A junction with another body was to have been formed in Branford. But having learned at Hartford, that Mr. Ingersol would be in town the next day to claim protection from the Assembly, they took quarters there, and kept out patrols during the whole night, to prevent his arrival without their knowledge. The succeeding morning they resumed their march, and met Mr. Ingersol in Wethersfield. They told him their business, and he, after some little hesitation, mounted on a round table, read his resignation.* That fin-

---

* The curious may be pleased to know that the resignation was expressed in these explicit terms:

Wethersfield, September 9th, 1765.
    I do hereby promise, that I never will receive any stamped papers which may arrive from Europe, in consequence of an act lately passed in the Parliament of Great-Britain; nor officiate as Stamp-Master or Distributer of Stamps, within the colony of Connecticut, either directly or indirectly. And I do

ished, the multitude desired him to cry out "liberty and property" three times; which he did, and was answered by three loud
huzzas. He then dined with some of the principal men at a tav-
ern, by whom he was treated with great politeness, and afterwards was escorted by about five hundred horse to Hartford,
where he again read his resignation amidst the unbounded ac-
clamations of the people. I have chosen to style this collection
the *yeomanry*, the *multitude*, or the *people*, because I could not
make use of the English word *mob*, which generally signifies a
disorderly concurrence of the rabble, without conveying an erroneous idea. It is scarcely necessary to add, that the people,
their objects being effected, without offering disturbance, dispersed to their homes.*

Colonel Putnam, who instigated the people to these measures, was prevented from attending by accident. But he was de-
puted soon after, with two other gentlemen, to wait on Governor Fitch on the same subject. The questions of the Governor,
and answers of Putnam, will serve to indicate the spirit of the

---

hereby notify to all the inhabitants of his Majesty's colony of Connecticut
(notwithstanding the said office or trust has been committed to me) not to
apply to me, ever after, for any stamped paper; *hereby declaring that I do resign
the said office*, and execute *these* PRESENTS of my own FREE WILL AND AC-
CORD, without any equivocation or mental reservation.

In witness whereof I have hereunto set my hand,

J. INGERSOL.

* To give a trait of the urbanity that prevailed, it may not be amiss to mention a jest that passed in the cavalcade to Hartford, and was received with the
most perfect good humour. Mr. Ingersol, who by chance rode a white horse,
being asked "What he thought, to find himself attended by such a retinue?"
replied, "that he had now a clearer idea than ever he had before conceived of
that passage in the Revelations, which describes *Death on a pale horse, and hell
following him.*"

times. After some conversation, the Governor asked, "What he should do if the stamped paper should be sent to him by the King's authority?" Putnam replied, "lock it up until we shall visit you again." "And what will you do then?" "We shall expect you to give us the key of the room in which it is deposited; and, if you think fit, in order to screen yourself from blame, you may forewarn us, upon our peril, not to enter the room." "And what will you do afterwards?" "Send it safely back again." "But if I should refuse admission?" "In such a case, your house will be levelled with the dust in five minutes." It was supposed, that a report of this conversation was one reason why the stamped paper was never sent from New-York to Connecticut.

Such unanimity in the Provincial Assemblies, and decision in the yeomanry, carried beyond the Atlantic a conviction of the inexpediency of attempting to enforce the new Revenue System. The Stamp Act being repealed, and the measures in a manner quieted, Colonel Putnam continued to labour with his own hands, at farming, without interruption, except, for a little time, by the loss of the first joint of his right thumb from one accident and the compound fracture of his right thigh from another: that thigh, being rendered nearly an inch shorter than the left, occasioned him ever to limp in his walk.

The Provincial officers and soldiers from Connecticut, who survived the conquest of the Havannah, appointed General Lyman to receive the remainder of their prize-money, in England. A company, composed partly of military, and partly of other gentlemen, whose object was to obtain from the Crown a grant of land on the Mississippi, also committed to him the negotiation of their affairs. When several years had elapsed in applications, a grant of land was obtained. In 1770, General Lyman, with Colonel Putnam, and two or three others, went to explore the situation. After a tedious voyage, and a laborious passage up the Mississippi, they accomplished their business.

General Lyman came back to Connecticut with the explorers, but soon returned to the Natchez: there formed an establishment and laid his bones. Colonel Putnam placed some labourers with provisions and farming utensils upon his location; but the increasing troubles shortly after ruined the prospect of deriving any advantage from that quarter.

In speaking of the troubles that ensued, I not only omit to say any thing on the obnoxious claim asserted in the British declaratory act, the continuation of the duty on tea, the attempt to obtrude that article upon the Americans, the abortion of this project, the Boston Port Bill, the alteration of the charter of Massachusetts, and other topics of universal notoriety; but even waive all discussion of irritations on the one part, and supplications on the other, which preceded the war between Great-Britain and her colonies on this continent. It will ever be acknowledged by those who were best acquainted with facts, and it should be made known to posterity, that the king of England had not, in his extensive dominions, subjects more loyal, more dutiful, or more zealous for his glory than the Americans; and that nothing short of a melancholy persuasion, that the "measures which for many years had been systematically pursued by his ministers, were calculated to subvert their constitutions," could have dissolved their powerful attachment to that kingdom which they fondly called their *parent country.* Here, without digression to develope the cause, or describe the progress, it may suffice to observe, the dispute now verged precipitately to an awful crisis. Most considerate men foresaw it would terminate in blood. But rather than suffer the chains, which they believed in preparation, to be rivetted, they nobly determined to sacrifice their lives. In vain did they deprecate the infatuation of those transatlantic counsels which drove them to deeds of desperation. Convinced of the rectitude of their cause, and doubtful of the issue, they felt the most painful solicitude for the fate of their country, on contemplating the superior strength of the nation with which it was to contend. America, thinly inhabited, under thirteen distinct colonial governments, could have little hope of success, but from the protection of providence, and the unconquerable spirit of freedom which pervaded the mass of the people. It is true, since the peace she had surprisingly increased in wealth and population; but the resources of Britain almost exceeded credibility or conception. It is not wonderful, then, that some good citizens, of weaker nerves, recoiled at the prospect; while others, who had been officers in the late war, or who had witnessed, by travelling, the force of Britain, stood aloof. All eyes were now turned to find the men who, possessed of military experience, would dare, in the approaching hour of severest trial, to lead their undisciplined fellow-citizens to battle. For none were so stupid as not to comprehend, that want of success would involve the leaders in the punishment of rebellion. Putnam was among the first and most conspicuous who stepped forth. Although the Americans had been, by many who wished their subjugation, indiscreetly as indiscriminately stigmatized with the imputation of cowardice—he felt—he knew for himself, he was no coward; and from what he had seen and known, he believed that his countrymen, driven to the extremity of defending their rights by arms, would find no difficulty in wiping away the ungenerous aspersion. As he happened to be often at Boston, he held many conversations, on these subjects, with General Gage, the British Commander in Chief, Lord Percy, Colonel Sheriff, Colonel Small, and many officers with whom he had formerly served, who were now at the Head-

Quarters. Being often questioned, "in case the dispute should proceed to hostilities, what part he would really take?" he always answered, "with his country; and that, let whatever might happen, he was prepared to abide the consequence." Being interrogated, "whether *he,* who had been a witness to the prowess and victories of the British fleets and armies, did not think them equal to the conquest of a country which was not the owner of a single ship, regiment, or magazine?" he rejoined, that

> he could only say, justice would be on our side, and the event with providence: but that he had calculated, if it required six years for the combined forces of England and her colonies, to conquer such a feeble country as Canada, it would, at least, take a very long time for England alone to overcome her own widely extended colonies, which were much stronger than Canada: That when men fought for every thing dear, in what they believed to be the most sacred of all causes, and in their own native land, they would have great advantages over their enemies, who were not in the same situation; and that, having taken into view all circumstances, for his own part, he fully believed that America would not be so easily conquered by England as those gentlemen seemed to expect.

Being once, in particular, asked, "whether he did not seriously believe that a well appointed British army of five thousand veterans could march through the whole continent of America?" he replied briskly, "no doubt, if they behaved civilly, and paid well for every thing they wanted; but"—after a moment's pause added—"if they should attempt it in a hostile manner (though the American men were out of the question) the women, with their ladles and broom-sticks, would knock them all on the head before they had got half way through." This was the tenor, our hero hath often told me, of these amicable interviews; and thus, as it commonly happens in disputes about future events which depend on opinion, they parted without conviction, no more to meet in a friendly manner, until after the appeal should have been made to Heaven, and the issue confirmed by the sword. In the mean time, to provide against the worst contingency, the militia in the several colonies was sedulously trained; and those select companies, the flower of our youth, which were denominated minutemen, agreeably to the indication of their name, held themselves in readiness to march at a moment's warning.

At length the fatal day arrived, when hostilities commenced. General Gage, in the evening of the 18th of April, 1775, detached from Boston, the grenadiers and light infantry of the army, commanded by Lieutenant-Colonel Smith, to destroy some military and other stores deposited by the province at Concord. About sunrise the next morning, the detachment, on marching into Lexington, fired upon a company of militia who had just re-assembled; for having been alarmed late at night, with reports that the regulars were advancing to demolish the stores, they collected on their parade, and were dismissed with orders to re-assemble at beat of drum. It is established by the affidavits of more than thirty persons who were present, that the first fire, which killed eight of the militia, then beginning to disperse, was given by the British, without provocation. The spark of war, thus kindled, ran with unexampled rapidity, and raged with unwonted violence. To repel the aggression, the people of the bordering towns spontaneously rushed to arms, and poured their scattering shot from every convenient station upon the regulars, who, after marching to Concord, and destroying the magazine, would have found their retreat intercepted, had they not been reinforced by Lord Percy, with the battalion companies of three regiments, and a body of marines. Notwithstanding the junction, they were hard pushed, and pursued until they could find protection from their ships. Of the British, two hundred and eighty-three were killed, wounded, and taken. The Americans had thirty-nine killed, nineteen wounded, and two made prisoners.

Nothing could exceed the celerity with which the intelligence flew every where, that blood had been shed by the British troops. The country, in motion, exhibited but one scene of hurry, preparation and revenge. Putnam, who was plowing when he heard the news, left his plough in the middle of the field, unyoked his team, and without waiting to change his clothes, set off for the theatre of action. But finding the British retreated to Boston, and invested by a sufficient force to watch their movements, he came back to Connecticut, levied a regiment, under authority of the legislature, and speedily returned to Cambridge.*

* An article, void of foundation, mentioning an interview between General Gage and General Putnam, appeared in the English Gazettes, in these words:

General Gage, viewing the American army with his telescope, saw General Putnam in it, which surprised him; and he contrived to get a message delivered to him, that he wanted to speak to him. Putnam, without any hesitation, waited upon him. General Gage showed him his fortifications, and advised him to lay down his arms. General Putnam replied, he could force his fortifications in half an hour, and advised General Gage to go on board the ships with his troops.

The apprehension of an attack is adduced with much more verisimilitude in M'Fingal, as the reason why General Gage would not suffer the inhabitants to go from the town of Boston, after he had promised to grant permission:

So Gage of late agreed, you know,
To let the Boston people go:

He was now promoted to be a Major-General on the Provincial staff, by his colony; and, in a little time, confirmed by Congress, in the same rank on the Continental establishment. General Ward, of Massachusetts, by common consent, commanded the whole; and the celebrated Dr. Warren was made a Major-General.

Not long after this period, the British Commander in Chief found the means to convey a proposal, privately, to General Putnam, that if he would relinquish the rebel party, he might rely upon being made a Major-General on the British establishment, and receiving a great pecuniary compensation for his services. General Putnam spurned at the offer; which, however, he thought prudent at that time to conceal from public notice.

It could scarcely have been expected, but by those credulous patriots who were prone to believe whatever they ardently desired, that officers assembled from colonies distinct in their manners and prejudices, selected from laborious occupations, to command a heterogeneous crowd of their equals, compelled to be soldiers only by the spur of occasion, should long be able to preserve harmony among themselves, and subordination among their followers. As the fact would be a phenomenon, the idea was treated with mirth and mockery by the friends to the British government. Yet this unshaken embryo of a military corps, composed of militia, minutemen, volunteers, and levies, with a burlesque appearance of multiformity in arms, accoutrements,

---

Yet when he saw, 'gainst troops that brav'd him,
They were the only guards that sav'd him,
Kept off that Satan of a *Putnam*,
From breaking in to maul and mutt'n him,
He'd too much wit such leagues t'observe,
And shut them in again to starve.
M'FINGAL. Canto I.

Israel Putnam leaving the plow to join the fight for independence

cloathing and conduct, at last grew into a regular army—an army which, having vindicated the rights of human nature, and established the independence of a new empire, merited and obtained the glorious distinction of the patriot army—the patriot army, whose praises for their fortitude in adversity, bravery in battle, moderation in conquest, perseverance in supporting the cruel extremities of hunger and nakedness without a murmur or sigh, as well as for their magnanimity in retiring to civil life, at the moment of victory, with their arms in their hands, and without any just compensation for their services, will only cease to be celebrated when time shall exist no more.

Enthusiasm for the cause of liberty, substituted in the place of discipline, not only kept these troops together, but enabled them at once to perform the duties of a disciplined army. Though the commanding officers from the four colonies of New-England were in a manner independent, they acted harmoniously in concert. The first attention had been prudently directed towards forming some little redoubts and intrenchments; for it was well known that lines, however slight or untenable, were calculated to inspire raw soldiers with a confidence in themselves. The next care was to bring the live stock from the islands in Boston bay, in order to prevent the enemy (already surrounded by land), from making use of them for fresh provisions. In the latter end of May, between two and three hundred men were sent to drive off the stock from Hog and Noddle islands, which are situated on the north-east side of Boston harbour. Advantage having been taken of the ebb-tide, when the water is fordable between the main and Hog-island, as it is between that and Noddle-island, the design was effected. But a skirmish ensued, in which some of the marines, who had been stationed to guard them, were killed: and as the firing

continued between the British water-craft and our party, a reinforcement of three hundred men, with two pieces of artillery,
was ordered to join the latter. General Putnam took the command, and having himself gone down on the beach, within con-
versing distance, and *ineffectually* ordered the people on board
an armed schooner to strike, he plied her with shot so furiously
that the crew made their escape, and the vessel was burnt. An
armed sloop was likewise so much disabled as to be towed off
by the boats of the fleet. Thus ended this affair, in which several
hundred sheep, and some cattle were removed from under the
muzzles of the enemy's cannon, and our men, accustomed to
stand fire, by being for many hours exposed to it, without meeting with any loss.

The Provincial Generals having received advice that the British Commander in Chief designed to take possession of the
heights on the peninsula of Charles-Town, detached a thousand men in the night of the 16th of June, under the orders of
General Warren, to intrench themselves upon one of these em-
inences, named Bunker-Hill. Though retarded by accidents,
from beginning the work until nearly midnight, yet, by dawn of
day, they had constructed a redoubt about eight rods square,
and commenced a breast-work from the left to the low grounds;
which an insufferable fire from the shipping, floating batteries,
and cannon on Cop's Hill, in Boston, prevented them from
completing. At mid-day four battalions of foot, ten companies
of grenadiers, ten companies of light-infantry, with a proportion of artillery, commanded by Major-General Howe, landed
under a heavy cannonade from the ships, and advanced in three
lines to the attack. The light-infantry being formed on the
right, was directed to turn the left flank of the Americans; and
the grenadiers, supported by two battalions, to storm the re-

doubt in front. Meanwhile, on application, these troops were augmented by the 47th regiment, the 1st battalion of marines, together with some companies of light-infantry and grenadiers, which formed an aggregate force of between two and three thousand men. But so difficult was it to reinforce the Americans, by sending detachments across the Neck, which was raked by the cannon of the shipping, that not more than fifteen hundred men were brought into action. Few instances can be produced in the annals of mankind, where soldiers, who never had before faced an enemy, or heard the whistling of a ball, behaved with such deliberate and persevering valour. It was not until after the grenadiers had been twice repulsed to their boats, General Warren slain, his troops exhausted of their ammunition, their lines in a manner enfiladed by artillery, and the redoubt half filled with British regulars, that the word was given to retire. In that forlorn condition, the spectacle was astonishing as new, to behold these undisciplined men, most of them without bayonets, disputing with the butt-end of their muskets against the British bayonet, and receding in sullen despair. Still the light-infantry on their left would certainly have gained their rear, and exterminated this gallant corps, had not a body of four hundred Connecticut men, with the Captains Knowlton and Chester, after forming a temporary breast-work, by pulling up one post-and-rail fence and putting it upon another, performed prodigies of bravery. They held the enemy at bay until the main body had relinquished the heights, and then retreated across the Neck with more regularity, and less loss, than could have been expected. The British, who effected nothing but the destruction of Charles-Town by a wanton conflagration, had more than one half of their whole number killed and wounded: the Americans only three hundred and fifty-five killed, wounded, and missing.

In this battle, the presence and example of General Putnam, who arrived with the reinforcement, were not less conspicuous than useful. He did every thing that an intrepid and experienced officer could accomplish. The enemy pursued to Winter-Hill— Putnam made a stand, and drove them back under cover of their ships.

The premature death of Warren, one of the most illustrious patriots that ever bled in the cause of freedom; the veteran appearance of Putnam, collected, yet ardent in action; together with the astonishing scenery and interesting group around Bunker-Hill, rendered this a magnificent subject for the historic pencil. Accordingly Trumbull, formerly an Aid-de-Camp to General Washington, afterwards Deputy-Adjutant-General of the northern army, now an artist of great celebrity in Europe, hath finished this picture with that boldness of conception, and those touches of art which demonstrate the master. Heightened in horror by the flames of a burning town, and the smoke of conflicting armies, the principal scene, taken the moment when Warren fell, represents that hero in the agonies of death, a grenadier on the point of bayoneting him, and Colonel Small, to whom he was familiarly known, arresting the soldier's arms; at the head of the British line, Major Pitcairne is seen falling dead into the arms of his son; and not far distant General Putnam is placed at the rear of our retreating troops, in the light blue and scarlet uniform he wore that day, with his head uncovered, and his sword waving towards the enemy, as it were to stop their impetuous pursuit. In nearly the same attitude he is exhibited by Barlow in that excellent poem, the Vision of Columbus.

There strides bold Putnam, and from all the plains
Calls the third host, the tardy rear sustains,

And, 'mid the whizzing deaths that fill the air,
Waves back his sword, and dares the foll'wing war.*

After this action, the British strongly fortified themselves on the peninsulas of Boston and Charles-Town; while the Provincials remained posted in the circumjacent country in such a manner as to form a blockade. In the beginning of July, General Washington, who had been constituted by Congress, Commander in Chief of the American forces, arrived at Cambridge, to take the command. Having formed the army into three grand divisions, consisting of about twelve regiments each, he appointed Major General Ward to command the right wing, Major-General Lee the left wing, and Major-General Putnam the reserve. General Putnam's alertness in accelerating the construction of the necessary defences was particularly noticed and highly approved by the Commander in Chief.

---

* The writer of this Essay had occasion of remarking, to the poet and the painter, while they were three thousand miles distant from each other, at which distance they had formed and executed the plans of their respective productions, the similarity observable in their descriptions of General Putnam. These *Chefs d'oeuvres* are mentioned not with a vain presumption of adding eclat of duration to works which have received the seal of immortality, but because they present, in the sister arts, the same illustrious action of our hero. I persuade myself I need not apologize for annexing the beautiful lines from the poem in question, on the death of General Warren.

> There, hapless Warren, thy cold earth was seen:
> There spring thy laurels in immortal green;
> Dearest of Chiefs that ever press'd the plain,
> In freedom's cause, with early honours, slain,
> Still dear in death, as when in fight you mov'd,
> By hosts applauded and by heav'n approv'd;
> The faithful muse shall tell the world thy fame,
> And unborn realms resound th' immortal name.

The Battle of Bunker (Breed's) Hill, fought June 17, 1775

About the 20th of July, the declaration of Congress, setting forth the reasons of their taking up arms, was proclaimed at the head of the several divisions. It concluded with these patriotic and noble sentiments:

> In our own native land, in defence of the freedom that is our birth-right, and which we ever enjoyed until the late violation of it; for the protection of our property, acquired solely by the honest industry of our forefathers and ourselves; against violence actually offered, we have taken up arms. We shall lay them down when hostilities shall cease on the part of the aggressors, and all danger of their being renewed shall be removed, and not before.
>
> With an humble confidence in the mercies of the supreme and impartial Judge and Ruler of the universe, we most devoutly implore his divine goodness to conduct us happily through this great conflict, to dispose our adversaries to reconciliation on reasonable terms, and, thereby, to relieve the empire from the calamities of civil war.

As soon as these memorable words were pronounced to General Putnam's division, which he had ordered to be paraded on Prospect-Hill, they shouted in three huzzas aloud, Amen! whereat (a cannon from the fort being fired as a signal) the new *Standard*, lately sent from Connecticut, was suddenly seen to rise and unroll itself to the wind. On one side was inscribed, in large letters of gold, "AN APPEAL TO HEAVEN," and on the other were delineated the armorial bearings of Connecticut, which, without supporters or crest, consist, unostentatiously, of *three Vines*, with this motto *"Qui transtulit, sustinet;"** alluding to the pious confidence our forefathers placed in the protec-

---

* Literally, *"He who transplanted them will support them."*

tion of Heaven, those three allegorical scions—KNOWLEDGE—LIBERTY—RELIGION—which they had been instrumental in transplanting to America.

The strength of position on the enemy's part, and want of ammunition on ours, prevented operations of magnitude from being attempted. Such diligence was used in fortifying our camps, and such precaution adopted to prevent surprise, as to ensure tranquillity to the troops during the winter. In the spring, a position was taken so menacing to the enemy, as to cause them, on the 17th of March, 1776, to abandon Boston, not without considerable precipitation and dereliction of royal stores.

As a part of the hostile fleet lingered for some time in Nantasket-Road, about nine miles below Boston, General Washington continued himself in Boston, not only to see the coast entirely clear, but also to make many indispensable arrangements. His Excellency, proposing to leave Major-General Ward, with a few regiments, to finish the fortifications intended as a security against an attack by water, in the mean time dispatched the greater part of the army to New-York, where it was most probable the enemy would make a descent. Upon the sailing of a fleet with troops in the month of January, Major-General Lee had been sent to the defence of that city; who, after having caused some works to be laid out, proceeded to follow that fleet to South-Carolina. The Commander in Chief was now exceedingly solicitous that these works should be completed as soon as possible, and accordingly gave the following

Orders and Instructions for Major-General Putnam.
As there are the best reasons to believe that the enemy's fleet and army, which left Nantasket-Road last Wednesday evening, are bound to New-York, to endeavour to possess that important post, and, if possible, to secure the com-

munication by Hudson's river to Canada, it must be our care to prevent them from accomplishing their designs. To that end I have detached Brigadier-General Heath, with the whole body of riflemen, and five battalions of the Continental army, by the way of Norwich, in Connecticut, to New-York. These, by an express arrived yesterday from General Heath, I have reason to believe, are in New-York. Six more battalions, under General Sullivan, march this morning by the same route, and will, I hope, arrive there in eight or ten days at farthest. The rest of the army will immediately follow in divisions, leaving only a convenient space between each division, to prevent confusion, and want of accommodation upon their march. You will, no doubt, make the best dispatch in getting to New-York. Upon your arrival there, you will assume the command, and immediately proceed in continuing to execute the *plan* proposed by Major-General Lee, for fortifying that city, and securing the passes of the East and North rivers. If, upon consultation with the Brigadiers General and Engineers, any alteration in that *plan* is thought necessary, you are at liberty to make it: cautiously avoiding to break in too much upon his main design, unless where it may be apparently necessary so to do, and that by the general voice and opinion of the gentlemen above-mentioned.

You will meet the Quarter-Master-General, Colonel Mifflin, and Commissary-General,* at New-York. As these are both men of excellent talents in their different departments, you will do well to give them all the authority and assistance they require: And should a council of war be necessary, it is my direction they assist at it.

---

* Colonel Joseph Trumbull, eldest son to the Governor of that name.

Your long service and experience will, better than my particular directions at this distance, point out to you the works most proper to be first raised; and your perseverance, activity, and zeal will lead you, without my recommending it, to exert every *nerve* to disappoint the enemy's designs.

Devoutly praying that the POWER which has hitherto sustained the American arms, may continue to bless them with the divine protection, I bid you—FAREWELL.

Given at Head-Quarters, in Cambridge, this twenty-ninth of March, 1776.

G. WASHINGTON.

Invested with these commands, General Putnam travelled by long and expeditious stages to New-York. His first precaution, upon his arrival, was to prevent disturbance, or surprise in the night season. With these objects in view, after posting the necessary guards, he issued his orders.* He instituted, likewise, other wholesome regulations to meliorate the police of the troops, and to preserve the good agreement that subsisted between them and the citizens.

Notwithstanding the war had now raged, in other parts, with unaccustomed severity for nearly a year, yet the British ships at

---

* GENERAL ORDERS.
Head-Quarters, New-York, April 5, 1776.
The soldiers are strictly enjoined to retire to their barracks and quarters at tattoo-beating, and to remain there until the reveille is beat.

Necessity obliges the General to desire the inhabitants of the city to observe the same rule, as no person will be permitted to pass any sentry after this night, without the countersign.

The inhabitants, whose business require it, may know the countersign, by applying to any of the Brigade-Majors.

New-York, one of which had once fired upon the town to intimidate the inhabitants, found the means of being supplied with fresh water and provisions. General Putnam resolved to adopt effectual measures for putting a period to this intercourse, and accordingly expressed his prohibition* in the most pointed terms.

Nearly at the same moment, a detachment of a thousand Continentals was sent to occupy Governor's Island, a regiment to fortify Red Hook, and some companies of riflemen to the Jersey shore. Of two boats, belonging to two armed vessels, which attempted to take on board fresh water from the watering-place on Staten Island, one was driven off by the riflemen, with two or three seamen killed in it, and the other captured with thirteen. A few days afterwards, Captain Vandeput, of the Asia man of war, the senior officer of the ships on this station, finding the intercourse with the shore interdicted, their limits contracted, and that no good purposes could be answered by remaining there, sailed, with all the armed vessels, out of the

---

* PROHIBITION.

Head-Quarters, New-York, April 8, 1776.

The General informs the inhabitants, that it is become absolutely necessary, that all communication between the ministerial fleet and the shore should be immediately stopped; for that purpose he has given positive orders, the ships should no longer be furnished with provisions. Any inhabitants, or others, who shall be taken that have been on board, after the publishing this order, or near any of the ships, or going on board, will be considered as enemies, and treated accordingly.

All boats are to sail from Beekman-slip. Captain James Alner is appointed inspector, and will give permits to oystermen. It is ordered and expected that none attempt going without a pass.

ISRAEL PUTNAM,

Major-General in the Continental Army, and Commander in Chief of the Forces in New-York.

harbour. These arrangements and transactions, joined to an un-remitting attention to the completion of the defenses, gave full scope to the activity of General Putnam, until the arrival of General Washington, which happened about the middle of April.

The Commander in Chief, in his first public orders,

complimented the officers who had successively commanded at New-York, and returned his thanks to them as well as to the officers and soldiers under their command, for the many works of defence which had been so expeditiously erected: at the same time he expressed an expectation that the same spirit of zeal for the service would continue to an-imate their future conduct.

Putnam, who was then the only Major-General with the main army, had still a chief agency in forwarding the fortifications, and, with the assistance of the Brigadiers Spencer and Lord Stirling, in assigning to the different corps their alarm posts.

Congress having intimated a desire of consulting with the Commander in Chief, on the critical posture of affairs, his Ex-cellency repaired to Philadelphia accordingly, and was absent from the twenty-first of May until the sixth of June. General Putnam, who commanded in that interval, had it in charge to open all letters directed to General Washington *on public ser-vice,* and, if important, after regulating his conduct by their con-tents, to forward them by express; to expedite the works then erecting; to begin others which were specified; to establish sig-nals for communicating an alarm; to guard against the possibil-ity of surprise; to secure well the powder-magazine; to augment, by every means in his power, the quantity of cartridges; and to send Brigadier-General Lord Stirling to put the posts in the *Highlands* into a proper condition of defence. He had also *a pri-*

vate and confidential instruction, to afford whatever aid might be required by the Provincial Congress of New-York, for apprehending certain of their disaffected citizens: and as it would be most convenient to take the detachment for this service from the troops on Long-Island, under the command of Brigadier-General Greene, it was recommended that this officer should be advised of the plan, and that the execution should be conducted with secrecy and celerity, as well as with decency and good order. In the records of the army are preserved the daily orders which were issued in the absence of the Commander in Chief, who, on his return, was not only satisfied that the works had been prosecuted with all possible dispatch, but also that the other duties had been properly discharged.

It was the latter end of June, when the British fleet, which had been at Halifax waiting for reinforcements from Europe, began to arrive at New-York. To obstruct its passage, some marine preparations had been made. General Putnam, to whom the direction of the whale-boats, fire-rafts, flat-bottomed boats, and armed vessels, was committed, afforded his patronage to a project for destroying the enemy's shipping by explosion. A *machine,* altogether different from any thing hitherto devised by the art of man, had been invented by Mr. David Bushnell,* for

* David Bushnell, A. M. of Saybrook, in Connecticut, invented several other machines for the annoyance of shipping; these, from accidents, not militating against the philosophical principles on which their success depended, only partially succeeded. He destroyed a vessel in the charge of Commodore Symmonds, whose report to the Admiral was published. One of his kegs also demolished a vessel near the Long-Island shore. About Christmas, 1777, he committed to the Delaware a number of kegs, destined to fall among the British fleet at Philadelphia; but his squadron of kegs, having been separated and retarded by the ice, demolished but a single boat. This catastrophe, however, produced an alarm, unprecedented in its nature and degree; which has been so

submarine navigation, which was found to answer the purpose perfectly, of rowing horizontally at any given depth under water, and of rising or sinking at pleasure. To *this machine,* called the American Turtle, was attached *a magazine of powder,* which it was intended to be fastened under the bottom of a ship, with a driving screw, in such sort, that the same stroke which disengaged it from the machine, should put the internal clock-work in motion. This being done, the ordinary operation of a gun-lock, at the distance of half an hour, an hour, or any determinate time, would cause the powder to explode, and leave the effects

---

happily described in the subsequent song, by the Hon. Francis Hopkinson, that the event it celebrates will not be forgotten, so long as mankind shall continue to be delighted with works of humour and taste.

THE BATTLE OF THE KEGS: —*A Song.*
Tune, Moggy Lawder.

Gallants, attend, and hear a friend
Thrill forth harmonious ditty:
Strange things I'll tell, which late befel
In Philadelphia city.

'Twas early day, as poets say,
Just when the sun was rising,
A soldier stood on log of wood,
And saw a sight surprising.

As in a maze he stood to gaze,
The truth can't be denied, Sir,
He spied a score of kegs or more,
Come floating down the tide, Sir.

A sailor, too, in jerkin blue,
The strange appearance viewing,
First damn'd his eyes, in great surprise,
Then said—"Some mischief's brewing.

to the common laws of nature. The simplicity, yet combination discovered in the mechanism of this wonderful machine, were acknowledged by those skilled in physics, and particularly hydraulics, to be not less ingenious than novel. The inventor, whose constitution was too feeble to permit him to perform the labour of rowing the Turtle, had taught his brother to manage it with perfect dexterity; but unfortunately his brother fell sick of a fever just before the arrival of the fleet. Recourse was therefore had to a sergeant in the Connecticut troops; who, having received whatever instructions could be communicated to him

---

"These Kegs now hold the rebels bold,
    Pack'd up like pickled herring;
And they're come down, t' attack the town
    In this new way of ferry'ng."

The soldier flew; the sailor too;
    And, scar'd almost to death, Sir,
Wore out their shoes, to spread the news,
    And ran till out of breath, Sir.

Now up and down, throughout the town,
    Most frantic scenes were acted;
And some ran here, and some ran there,
    Like men almost distracted.

Some fire cried, which some denied,
    But said the earth had quaked:
And girls and boys, with hideous noise,
    Ran through the town half naked.

Sir William* he, snug as a flea,
    Lay all this time a snoring;
Nor dreamt of harm, as he lay warm
    In bed with Mrs. L*r*ng.

* Sir William Howe.

84

in a short time, went, too late in the night, with all the apparatus, under the bottom of the Eagle, a sixty-four gun ship, on
board of which the British Admiral, Lord Howe, commanded.
In coming up, the screw that had been calculated to perforate
the copper sheathing, unluckily struck against some iron plates
where the rudder is connected with the stern. This accident,

———

> Now in a fright, he starts upright,
>   Awak'd by such a clatter:
> He rubs both eyes, and boldly cries,
>   "For God's sake, what's the matter?"
>
> At his bedside he then espied
>   Sir Erskine* at command, Sir;
> Upon one foot he had one boot,
>   And t' other in his hand, Sir.
>
> "Arise! arise!" Sir Erskine cries;
>   "The rebels—more's the pity—
> Without a boat, are all on float,
>   And rang'd before the city."
>
> "The motley crew, in vessels new,
>   With Satan for their guide, Sir,
> Pack'd up in bags, or wooden kegs,
>   Come driving down the tide, Sir:
>
> "Therefore prepare for bloody war;
>   These kegs must all be routed,
> Or surely we despis'd shall be,
>   And British courage doubted."
>
> The Royal band now ready stand,
>   All rang'd in dread array, Sir,
> With stomachs stout, to see it out,
>   And make a bloody day, Sir.

* Sir William Erskine.

added to the strength of the tide which prevailed, and the want of adequate skill in the sergeant, occasioned such delay, that the dawn began to appear, whereupon he abandoned the magazine to chance, and after gaining a proper distance, for the sake of expedition, rowed on the surface towards the town. General

———

> The cannons roar from shore to shore,
>   The small arms make a rattle:
> Since wars began, I'm sure no man
>   E'er saw so strange a battle.
>
> The rebel* vales, the rebel dales,
>   With rebel trees surrounded,
> The distant woods, the hills and floods,
>   With rebel echoes sounded.
>
> The fish below swam to and fro,
>   Attack'd from ev'ry quarter;
> "Why sure," thought they, "the Devil's to pay
>   'Mong'st folks above the water."
>
> The kegs, 'tis said, though strongly made
>   Of rebel staves and hoops, Sir,
> Could not oppose their pow'rful foes,
>   The conqu'ring British troops, Sir.
>
> From morn to night those men of might
>   Display'd amazing courage;
> And when the sun was fairly down,
>   Retir'd to sup their porridge.
>
> An hundred men, with each a pen,
>   Or more, upon my word, Sir,
> It is most true, would be too few
>   Their valour to record, Sir.

* The British officers were so fond of the word *rebel*, that they often applied it most absurdly.

86

Putnam, who had been on the wharf anxiously expecting the result, from the first glimmering of light, beheld the machine near Governor's-Island, and sent a whale-boat to bring it on shore. In about twenty minutes afterwards the magazine exploded, and blew a vast column of water to an amazing height in the air. As the whole business had been kept an inviolable secret, he was not a little diverted with the various conjectures, whether this stupendous noise was produced by a bomb, a meteor, a water-spout, or an earthquake. Other operations of a most serious nature rapidly succeeded, and prevented a repetition of the experiment.

On the twenty-second day of August, the van of the British landed on Long-Island, and was soon followed by the whole army, except one brigade of Hessians, a small body of British, and some convalescents, left on Staten-Island. Our troops on Long-Island had been commanded during the summer by General Greene, who was now sick; and General Putnam took the command but two days before the battle of Flatbush. The instructions to him, pointing in the first place to decisive expedients suppressing the scattering, unmeaning, and wasteful fire of our men, contained regulations for the service of the guards, the Brigadiers and the Field-officers of the day; for the appoint-

---

> Such feats did they perform that day,
> Upon those wicked kegs, Sir.
> That years to come, if they get home,
> They'll make their boasts and brags, Sir.

Mr. Bushnell, having been highly recommended for his talents by President Stiles, General Parsons, and some other gentlemen of science, was appointed a Captain in the corps of sappers and miners; in which capacity he continued to serve with that corps until the conclusion of the war.

ment and encouragement of proper scouts, as well as for keeping the men constantly at their posts; for preventing the burning of buildings, except it should be necessary for military purposes, and for preserving private property from pillage and destruction. To these regulations were added, in a more diffuse, though not less spirited and professional stile, reflections on the distinction of an army from a mob; with exhortations for the soldiers to conduct themselves manfully in such a cause, and for their Commander to oppose the enemy's approach with detachments of his best troops; while he should endeavour to render their advance more difficult by constructing abbatis, and to entrap their parties by forming ambuscades. General Putnam was within the lines, when an engagement took place on the 27th, between the British army and our advanced corps, in which we lost about a thousand men in killed and missing, with the General Sullivan and Lord Stirling made prisoners. But our men, though attacked on all sides, fought with great bravery; and the enemy's loss was not light.

The unfortunate battle of Long-Island, the masterly retreat from thence, and the actual passage of part of the hostile fleet in the East-River, above the town, precluded the evacuation of New-York. A promotion of four Major-Generals, and six Brigadiers, had previously been made by Congress. After the retreat from Long-Island, the main army, consisting, for the moment, of sixty battalions, of which twenty were Continental, the residue levies and militia, was, conformably to the exigencies of the service, rather than to the rules of war, formed into fourteen brigades. Major-General Putnam commanded the right grand division of five brigades, the Majors-General Spencer and Greene the centre of six brigades, and Major-General Heath the left, which was posted near Kings-bridge, and composed of two brigades. The whole never amounted to twenty thousand effective men; while the British and German forces, under Sir William Howe, exceeded twenty-two thousand: indeed, the minister had asserted in parliament, that they would consist of more than thirty thousand. Our two centre divisions, both commanded by General Spencer, in the sickness of General Greene, moved towards Mount Washington, Harlaem Heights, and Horn's Hook, as soon as the final resolution was taken in a council of war, on the twelfth of September, to abandon the city. That event, thus circumstanced, took effect a few days after.

On Sunday, the fifteenth, the British, after sending three ships of war up the North-River, to Bloomingdale, and keeping up, for some hours, a severe cannonade on our lines, from those already in the East-River, landed in force, at Turtle Bay. Our new levies, commanded by a State Brigadier-General, fled without making resistance. Two brigades of General Putnam's division, ordered to their support, notwithstanding the exertion of their Brigadiers, and of the Commander in Chief himself, who came up at the instant, conducted themselves in the same shameful manner. His Excellency then ordered the Heights of Harlaem, a strong position, to be occupied. Thither the forces in the vicinity, as well as the fugitives, repaired. In the mean time General Putnam, with the remainder of his command, and the ordinary out-posts, was in the city. After having caused the brigades to begin their retreat by the route of Bloomingdale, in order to avoid the enemy, who were then in the possession of the main road leading to Kings-bridge, he gallopped to call off the pickets and guards. Having myself been a volunteer in his division, and acting Adjutant to the last regiment that left the city, I had frequent opportunities, that day, of beholding him, for the purpose of issuing orders, and encouraging the troops, flying, on his horse covered with foam, wherever his presence was most necessary. Without his extraordinary exertions, the guards must have been inevitably lost, and it is probable the entire corps would have been cut in pieces. When we were not far from Bloomingdale, an Aid-de-camp came from him at full speed, to inform that a column of British infantry was descending upon our right. Our rear was soon fired upon, and the Colonel of our regiment, whose order was just communicated for the front to file off to the left, was killed on the spot. With no other loss we joined the army, after dark, on the Heights of Harlaem.

Before our brigades came in, we were given up for lost by all our friends, so critical indeed was our situation, and so narrow the gap by which we escaped, that the instant we had passed the enemy closed it by extending their line from river to river. Our men, who had been fifteen hours under arms, harassed by marching and countermarching, in consequence of incessant alarms, exhausted as they were by heat and thirst, (for the day proved insupportably hot, and few or none had canteens, insomuch, that some died at the brooks where they drank) if attacked, could have made but feeble resistance.

If we take into consideration the debilitating sickness which weakened almost all our troops, the hard duty by which they were worn down in constructing numberless defences, the continual want of rest they had suffered since the enemy landed, in guarding from nocturnal surprise, the despondency infused into their minds by an insular situation, and a consciousness of inferiority to the enemy in discipline, together with the disadvantageous term upon which, in their state of separation, they might have been forced to engage; it appears highly probable that day would have presented an easy victory to the British. On the other side, the American Commander in Chief had wisely countenanced an opinion, then universally credited, that our army was three times more numerous than it was in reality. It is not a subject for astonishment, that the British, ignorant of the

existing circumstances, imposed upon as to the numbers by reports, and recollecting what a few brave men, slightly entrenched, had performed at Bunker-Hill, should proceed with
great circumspection. For their reproaches, that the rebels, as
they affected to style us, loved digging better than fighting, and
that they earthed themselves in holes like foxes, but ill concealed at the bottom of their own hearts the profound impression that action had made. Cheap and contemptible as we had
once seemed in their eyes, it had taught them to hold us in some
respect. This respect, in conjunction with a fixed belief, that the
enthusiastic spirit of our opposition must soon subside, and that
the inexhaustible resources of Britain would ultimately triumph,
without leaving any thing to chance (not the avarice or treachery of the British General, as the factious of his own nation
wished to insinuate), retarded their operation and afforded us
leisure to rescue from annihilation the miserable relics of an
army, hastening to dissolution by the expiration of enlistments,
and the country itself from irretrievable subjugation. IN
TRUTH, WE ARE NOT LESS INDEBTED TO THE MAT-
TOCK AT ONE PERIOD, THAN TO THE MUSKET AT AN-
OTHER, FOR OUR POLITICAL SALVATION. It required
great talents to determine when one or the other was most prof-
itably to be employed. I am aware how fashionable it has become to compare the American Commander in Chief, for the
prudence displayed in those dilatory and defensive operations,
so happily prosecuted in the early stages of the war, to the illustrious Roman, who acquired immortality in restoring the Com-
monwealth *by delay*. Advantageous and flattering as the comparison at first appears, it will be found, on examination, to stint
the American Fabius to the smaller moiety of his merited fame.
Did HE not, in scenes of almost unparalleled activity, discover
specimens of transcendent abilities; and might it not be proved,

to professional men, that boldness in council, and rapidity in execution, were, at least, equally with prudent procrastination, and the quality of not being compelled to action, attributes of his military genius? *This,* however, was an occasion, as apparent as pressing, for attaining his object *by delay.* From that he had everything to gain, nothing to lose. Yet there were not wanting *politicians,* AT THIS VERY TIME, who querulously blamed these *Fabian* measures, and loudly clamoured that the immense labour and expense bestowed on the fortification of New-York, had been thrown away; that if we could not face the enemy *there* after so many preparations, we might as well relinquish the contest at once, for we could no where make a stand; and that if General Washington, with an army of sixty thousand men, strongly entrenched, declined fighting with Sir William Howe, who had little more than one third of that number, it was not to be expected he would find any other occasion that might induce him to engage. But General Washington, content to suffer a temporary sacrifice of personal reputation, for the sake of securing a permanent advantage to his country, and regardless of those idle clamours for which he had furnished materials, by making his countrymen, in order the more effectually to make his enemy believe his force much greater than it actually was, inflexibly pursued his system, and gloriously demonstrated how poor and pitiful, in the estimation of A GREAT MIND, are the censorious strictures of those novices in war and politics, who, with equal rashness and impudence, presume to decide dogmatically on the merit of plans they could neither originate or comprehend!

That night our soldiers, excessively fatigued by the sultry march of the day, their clothes wet by a severe shower of rain that succeeded towards the evening, their blood chilled by the cold wind that produced a sudden change in the temperature of the air, and their hearts sunk within them by the loss of baggage, artillery, and works in which they had been taught to put great confidence, lay upon their arms, covered only by the clouds of an uncomfortable sky. To retrieve our disordered affairs, and prevent the enemy from profiting by them, no exertion was relaxed, no vigilance remitted on the part of our higher officers. The regiments which had been least exposed to fatigue that day, furnished the necessary picquets to secure the army from surprise. Those whose military lives had been short and unpractised, felt enough besides lassitude of body to disquiet the tranquillity of their repose. Nor had those who were older in service, and of more experience, any subject for consolation. The warmth of enthusiasm seemed to be extinguished. The force of discipline had not sufficiently occupied its place to give men a dependence upon each other. We were apparently about to reap the bitter fruits of that jealous policy, which some leading men, with the best motives, had sown in our federal councils, when they caused the mode to be adopted, for carrying on the war by detachments of militia, from apprehension that an established Continental army, after defending the country against foreign invasion, might subvert its liberties themselves. Paradoxical as it will appear, it may be profitable to be known to posterity, that while our very existence as an independent people was in question, the patriotic jealousy for the safety of our future *freedom* had been carried to such a virtuous but dangerous excess, as well nigh to preclude the attainment of our Independence. Happily that limited and hazardous system soon gave room to one more enlightened and salutary. This may be attributed to the reiterated arguments, the open remonstrances, and the confidential communications of the Commander in Chief; who, though not apt to despair of the Republic, on this occasion, expressed himself in terms of unusual despondency. He declared, in his letters, that he found, to his utter astonishment and mortification, that no reliance could be placed on a great proportion of his present troops, and that, unless efficient measures for establishing a permanent force should be speedily pursued, we had every reason to fear the final ruin of our cause.

Next morning several parties of the enemy appeared upon the plains in our front. On receiving this intelligence, General Washington rode quickly to the out-posts, for the purpose of preparing against an attack, if the enemy should advance with that design. Lieutenant-Colonel Knowlton's rangers, a fine selection from the eastern regiments, who had been skirmishing with an advanced party, came in, and informed the General that a body of British were under cover of a small eminence at no considerable distance. His Excellency, willing to raise our men from their dejection by the splendour of some little success, ordered Lieutenant-Colonel Knowlton, with his rangers, and Major Leitch, with three companies of Weedon's regiment of Virginians, to gain their rear; while appearances should be made of an attack in front. As soon as the enemy saw the party sent to decoy them, they ran precipitately down the hill, took possession of some fences and bushes, and commenced a brisk firing at long shot. Unfortunately Knowlton and Leitch made their onset rather in flank than in rear. The enemy changed their front, and the skirmish at once became close and warm. Major Leitch* having received three balls through his side, was soon borne from the field; and Colonel Knowlton, who had distinguished himself so gallantly at the battle of Bunker-Hill, was mortally wounded immediately after. Their men, however, undaunted by these disasters, stimulated with the thirst of revenge for the loss of their leaders, and, conscious of acting under the

---

* Major Leitch, after languishing some days, died of a locked jaw.

eye of the Commander in Chief, maintained the conflict with uncommon spirit and perseverance. But the General, seeing them in need of support, advanced part of the Maryland regiments of Griffith and Richardson, together with some detachments from such eastern corps as chanced to be most contiguous to the place of action. Our troops this day, without exception, behaved with the greatest intrepidity. So bravely did they repulse the British, that Sir William Howe moved his *reserve*, with two field pieces, a battalion of Hessian grenadiers, and a company of Chasseurs, to succour his retreating troops. General Washington, not willing to draw on a general action, declined pressing the pursuit. In this engagement were the second and third battalions of light infantry, the forty-second British regiment, and the German Chasseurs, of whom eight officers, and upwards of seventy privates were wounded, and our people buried nearly twenty, who were left dead on the field. We had about forty wounded: our loss in killed, except of two valuable officers, was very inconsiderable.

An advantage,* so trivial in itself, produced, in event, a surprising and almost incredible effect upon the whole army.

---

* A transcript from General Washington's Public Orders of the seventeenth will, better than any other document that could be adduced, show his sentiment on the conduct of the two preceding days, and how fervently he wished to foster the good dispositions discovered on the last.

ORDERS.
Head-Quarters, Harlaem Heights, September 17, 1776.
Parole, *Leitch.* Countersign, *Virginia.*

The General most heartily thanks the troops commanded yesterday by Major Leitch, who first advanced upon the enemy, and the others who so resolutely supported them. The behaviour yesterday was such a contrast to that of some of the troops the day before, as must show what may be done where officers and soldiers will exert themselves. Once more, therefore, the General

Amongst the troops not engaged, who, during the action, were throwing earth from the new trenches, with an alacrity that indicated a determination to defend them, every visage was seen to brighten, and to assume, instead of the gloom of despair, the glow of animation. This change, no less sudden than happy, left little room to doubt that the men, who ran the day before at the sight of an enemy, would now, to wipe away the stain of that disgrace, and to recover the confidence of their General, have conducted themselves in a very different manner. Some alteration was made in the distribution of corps to prevent the British from gaining either flank in the succeeding night. General Putnam, who commanded on the right, was directed in orders, in case the enemy should attempt to force the pass, to apply for a reinforcement to General Spencer, who commanded on the left.

General Putnam, who was too good an husbandman himself not to have a respect for the labours and improvements of others, strenuously seconded the views of the Commander in Chief in preventing the devastation of farms, and the violation of private property. For under pretext that the property in this quarter belonged to friends to the British government, as indeed it mostly did, a spirit of rapine and licentiousness began to prevail, which, unless repressed in the beginning, foreboded, besides the subversion of discipline, the disgrace and defeat of our arms.

---

calls upon officers and men, to act up to the noble cause in which they are engaged, and to support the *honour* and *liberties* of their country.

The gallant and brave Colonel Knowlton, who would have been an honour to any country, having fallen yesterday, while gloriously fighting, Captain Brown is to take the command of the party lately led by Colonel Knowlton. Officers and men are to obey him accordingly.

Our new defences now becoming so strong as not to admit insult with impunity, and Sir William Howe, not choosing to place too much at risk in attacking us in front, on the 12th day of October, leaving Lord Piercy with one Hessian and two British brigades, in his lines at Harlaem, to cover New-York, embarked with the main body of his army, with an intention of landing at *Frog's Neck*, situated near the town of West-Chester, and little more than a league above the communication called King's-bridge, which connects New-York island with the main. There was nothing to oppose him; and he effected his debarkation by nine o'clock in the morning. The same policy of keeping our army as compact as possible; the same system of avoiding being forced to action; and the same precaution to prevent the interruption of supplies, reinforcements or retreat, that lately dictated the evacuation of New-York, now induced General Washington to move towards the strong grounds in the upper part of West-Chester county.

About the same time General Putnam was sent to the western side of the Hudson, to provide against an irruption into the Jerseys, and soon after to Philadelphia, to put that town into a posture of defence. Thither I attend him, without stooping to dilate on the subsequent incidents, that might swell a folio, though here compressed to a single paragraph; without attempting to give in detail the skilful retrograde movements of our Commander in Chief, who, after detaching a garrison for Fort Washington, by pre-occupying with extemporaneous redoubts and entrenchments, the ridges from *Mile-Square* to *White-Plains*, and by folding one brigade behind another, in rear of those ridges that run parallel with the *Sound*, brought off all his artillery, stores, and sick, in the face of a superior foe; without commenting on the partial and equivocal battle fought near the last mentioned village, or the cause why the British, then in full force, (for the last of the Hessian infantry and British light-horse had just arrived) did not more seriously endeavour to in-duce a general engagement; without journalizing their military manoeuvres in falling back to King's-bridge, capturing Fort Washington, Fort Lee, and marching through the Jerseys; with-out enumerating the instances of rapine, murder, lust, and dev-astation, that marked their progress, and filled our bosoms with horror and indignation; without describing how a division of our dissolving army, with General Washington, was driven be-fore them beyond the Delaware; without painting the naked and forlorn condition of these much injured men, amidst the rigours of an inclement season; and without even sketching the consternation that seized the States at this perilous period, when General Lee, in leading from the north a small reinforce-ment to our troops, was himself taken prisoner by surprise; when every thing seemed decidedly declining to the last ex-tremity, and when every prospect but served to augment the de-pression of despair—until the genius of one man, in one day, at a single stroke, wrested from the veteran battalions of Britain and Germany the fruits acquired by the total operations of a successful campaign, and re-animated the expiring hope of a whole nation, by the glorious enterprize at Trenton.

While the hostile forces, rashly inflated with pride by a series of uninterrupted successes, and fondly dreaming that a period would soon be put to their labours, by the completion of their conquests, had been pursuing the wretched remnants of a dis-banded army to the banks of the Delaware, General Putnam was diligently employed in fortifying Philadelphia, the capture of which appeared indubitably to be their principal object. Here, by authority and example, he strove to conciliate contending factions, and to excite the citizens to uncommon efforts in de-fence of every thing interesting to freemen. His personal industry was unparalleled. His orders,* with respect to extinguishing accidental fires, advancing the public works, as well as in regard to other important objects, were perfectly military and proper. But his health was, for a while, impaired by his unrelaxed exertions.

The Commander in Chief having, in spite of all obstacles, made good his retreat over the Delaware, wrote to General Putnam from his Camp above the Falls of Trenton, on the very day he re-crossed the river to surprise the Hessians, expressing his satisfaction at the re-establishment of that General's health, and informing, that if he had not himself been well convinced before of the enemy's intention to possess themselves of Philadelphia, as soon as the frost should form ice strong enough to transport them and their artillery across the Delaware, he had now obtained an intercepted letter which placed the matter beyond a doubt. He added, that if the citizens of Philadelphia had any regard for the town, not a moment's time was to be lost until it should be put in the best possible posture of defence; but

---

* As a specimen, the following is preserved:

GENERAL ORDERS.

Head-Quarters, Philadelphia, December 14, 1776.

Colonel Griffin is appointed Adjutant-General to the troops in and about this city. All orders from the General, through him, either written or verbal, are to be strictly attended to and punctually obeyed.

In case of an alarm of fire, the city guards and patroles are to suffer the inhabitants to pass, unmolested, at any hour of the night; and the good people of Philadelphia are earnestly requested and desired to give every assistance in their power, with engines and buckets, to extinguish the fire. And as the Congress have ordered the city to be defended to the last extremity, the General hopes that no person will refuse to give every assistance possible to complete the fortifications that are to be erected in and about the city.

ISRAEL PUTNAM.

lest that should not be done, he directed the removal of all public stores, except provisions necessary for immediate use, to places of greater security. He queried whether, if a party of militia could be sent from Philadelphia to support those in the Jerseys, about Mount-Holly, it would not serve to save them from submission? At the same time he signified, as his opinion, the expediency of sending an active and influential officer to inspirit the people, to encourage them to assemble in arms, as well as to keep those already in arms from disbanding; and concluded by manifesting a wish that Colonel Forman, whom he desired to see for this purpose, might be employed on the service.

The enemy had vainly, as incautiously, imagined that to overrun was to conquer. They had even carried their presumption on our extreme weakness, and expected submission so far as to attempt covering the country through which they had marched with an extensive chain of cantonments. That link, which the post at Trenton supplied, consisted of a Hessian brigade of infantry, a company of Chasseurs, a squadron of light dragoons, and six field pieces. At eight o'clock in the morning of the twenty-sixth of December, General Washington, with twenty-four hundred men, came upon them, after they had paraded, took one thousand prisoners, and re-passed the same day, without loss, to his encampment. As soon as the troops were recovered from their excessive fatigue, General Washington re-crossed a second time to Trenton. On the second of January, Lord Cornwallis, with the bulk of the British army, advanced upon him, cannonaded his post, and offered him battle: but the two armies being separated by the interposition of Trenton Creek, General Washington had it in his option to decline an engagement, which he did for the sake of striking the masterly stroke that he then meditated. Having kindled frequent fires around his camp, posted faithful men to keep them burning, and advanced sentinels, whose fidelity might be relied upon, he decamped silently after dark, and, by a circuitous route, reached Princeton at nine o'clock the next morning. The noise of the firing, by which he killed and captured between five and six hundred of the British brigade in that town, was the first notice Lord Cornwallis had of this stolen march. General Washington, the project successfully accomplished, instantly filed off for the mountainous grounds of Morris-Town. Meanwhile, his Lordship, who arrived, by a forced march, at Princeton, just as he had left it, finding the Americans could not be overtaken, proceeded, without halting, to Brunswick.

On the fifth of January, 1777, from Pluckemin, General Washington dispatched an account of this second success to General Putnam, and ordered him to move immediately, with all his troops, to Crosswick's, for the purpose of co-operating in recovering the Jerseys; an event which the present fortunate juncture, while the enemy were yet panic-struck, appeared to promise. The General cautioned him, however, if the enemy should still continue at Brunswick, to guard with great circumspection against a surprise; especially as they, having recently suffered by two attacks, could scarcely avoid being edged with resentment to attempt retaliation. His Excellency farther advised him to give out his strength to be twice as great as it was; to forward on all the baggage and scattering men belonging to the division destined for Morris-Town; to employ as many spies as he should think proper; to keep a number of horsemen, in the dress of the country, going constantly, backwards and forwards on the same secret service; and, lastly, if he should discover any intention or motion of the enemy that could be depended upon, and might be of consequence, not to fail in conveying the intelligence, as rapidly as possible by express, to Head-Quarters. Major-General Putnam was directed soon after to take post at Princeton, where he continued until the spring. He had never with him more than a few hundred troops, though he was only at fifteen miles distance from the enemy's strong garrison of Brunswick. At one period, from a sudden diminution, occasioned by the tardiness of the militia turning out to replace those whose time of service was expired, he had fewer men for duty than he had miles of frontier to guard. Nor was the Commander in Chief in a more eligible situation. It is true, that while he had scarcely the semblance of an army, under the specious parade of a park of artillery, and the imposing appearance of his Head-Quarters, established at Morris-Town, he kept up, in the eyes of his countrymen, as well as in the opinion of his enemy, the appearance of no contemptible force. Future generations will find difficulty in conceiving how a handful of new-levied men and militia, who were necessitated to be inoculated for the small-pox in the course of the winter, could be subdivided and posted so advantageously, as effectually to protect the inhabitants, confine the enemy, curtail their forage, and beat up their quarters, without sustaining a single disaster.

In the battle of Princeton, Captain M'Pherson, of the 17th British regiment, a very worthy Scotchman, was desperately wounded in the lungs, and left with the dead. Upon General Putnam's arrival there, he found him languishing in extreme distress, without a surgeon, without a single accommodation, and without a friend to solace the sinking spirit in the gloomy hour of death. He visited, and immediately caused every possible comfort to be administered to him. Captain M'Pherson, who contrary to all appearances, recovered, after having demonstrated to General Putnam the dignified sense of obligations which a generous mind wishes not to conceal, one day, in familiar conversation, demanded, "Pray, Sir, what countryman are you?" "An American," answered the latter. "Not a Yankee?" said the other. "A full-blooded one," replied the General. "By G—d, I am sorry for that," rejoined M'Pherson, "I did not think there could be so much goodness and generosity in an American, or, indeed, in any body but a Scotchman."

While the recovery of Captain M'Pherson was doubtful, he desired that General Putnam would permit a friend in the British army at Brunswick to come and assist him in making HIS WILL. General Putnam, who had then only fifty men in his whole command, was sadly embarrassed by the proposition. On the one hand, he was not content that a British officer should have an opportunity to spy out the weakness of his post; on the other, it was scarcely in his nature to refuse complying with a dictate of humanity. He luckily bethought himself of an expedient which he hastened to put in practice. A flag of truce was dispatched with Captain M'Pherson's request, but under an injunction not to return with his friend until after dark. In the evening lights were placed in all the rooms of the College, and in every apartment of the vacant houses throughout the town. During the whole night, the fifty men, sometimes altogether, and sometimes in small detachments, were marched from different quarters by the house in which M'Pherson lay. Afterwards it was known that the officer who came on the visit, at his return, reported that General Putnam's army, upon the most moderate calculation, could not consist of less than four or five thousand men.

This winter's campaign, for our troops constantly kept the field after regaining a footing in the Jerseys, has never yet been faithfully and feelingly described. The sudden restoration of our cause from the very verge of ruin was interwoven with such a tissue of inscrutable causes and extraordinary events, that, fearful of doing the subject greater injustice, by a passing disquisition than a purposed silence, I leave it to the leisure of abler pens. The ill policy of the British doubtless contributed to accelerate this event. For the manner, impolitic as inhuman, in which they managed their temporary conquests, tended evidently to alienate the affections of their adherents, to confirm the wavering in an opposite interest, to rouse the supine into activity, to assemble the dispersed to the standard of America, and to infuse a spirit of revolt into the minds of those men who had, from necessity, submitted to their power. Their conduct in warring with fire and sword against the imbecility of youth, and the decrepitude of age; against the arts, the sciences, the curious inventions, and the elegant improvements in civilized life; against the melancholy widow, the miserable orphan, the peaceable professor of humane literature, and the sacred minister of the gospel, seemed to operate as powerfully, as if purposely intended to kindle the dormant spark of resistance into an inextinguishable flame. If we add to the black catalogue of provocations already enumerated, their insatiable rapacity in plundering friends and foes indiscriminately; their libidinous brutality in violating the chastity of the female sex; their more than Gothic rage in defacing private writings, public records, libraries of learning, dwellings of individuals, edifices for education, and temples of the Deity; together with their insufferable ferocity, unprecedented indeed among civilized nations, in murdering on the field of battle the wounded while begging for mercy, in causing their prisoners to famish with hunger and cold in prisons and prison ships, and in carrying their malice beyond death itself, by denying the decent rites of sepulture to the dead; we shall not be astonished that the yeomanry in the two Jerseys, when the first glimmering of hope began to break in upon them, rose as one man, with the unalterable resolution to perish in the generous cause, or expel their merciless invaders.

The principal officers, stationed at a variety of well-chosen, and at some almost inaccessible positions, seemed all to be actuated by the same soul, and only to vie with each other in giving proofs of vigilance, enterprise and valour. From what has been said respecting the scantiness of our aggregate force, it will be concluded, that the number of men, under the orders of each, was indeed very small. But the uncommon alertness of the troops, who were incessantly hovering round the enemy in scouts, and the constant communication they kept between the several stations most contiguous to each other, agreeably to the instructions* of the General in Chief, together with their read-

---

* The annexed private orders to Lord Stirling will show, in a laconic and military manner, the system of service then pursued:

To Brigadier-General Lord STIRLING.

MY LORD,

You are to repair to Baskenridge, and take upon you the command of the troops now there, and such as may be sent to your care.

You are to endeavour, as much as possible, to harass and annoy the enemy, by keeping scouting parties constantly, or as frequently as possible, around their quarters.

As you will be in the neighbourhood of Generals Dickenson and Warner, I recommend it to you to keep up a correspondence with them, and endeavour to regulate your parties by theirs, so as to have some constantly out.

Use every means in your power to obtain intelligence from the enemy; which may possibly be better effected by engaging some of those people who have obtained *Protections* to go in, under pretence of asking advice, than by any other means.

You will also use every means in your power to obtain and communicate the earliest accounts of the enemy's movements; and to assemble, in the speediest manner possible, your troops either for offence or defence.

Given at Head-Quarters, the fourth day of February, 1777.

GEO. WASHINGTON.

105

iness in giving, and confidence of receiving such reciprocal aid as the exigencies might require, served to supply the defect of force.

This manner of doing duty not only put our own posts beyond the reach of sudden insult and surprise, but so exceedingly harassed and intimidated the enemy, that foragers were seldom sent out by them, and never except in very large parties. General Dickenson, who commanded on General Putnam's left, discovered, about the 20th of January, a foraging party, consisting of about four hundred men, on the opposite side of the *Mill-Stone,* two miles from Somerset court-house. As the bridge was possessed and defended by three field-pieces, so that it could not be passed, General Dickenson, at the head of four hundred militia, broke the ice, crossed the river where the water was about three feet deep, resolutely attacked, and totally defeated the foragers. Upon their abandoning the convoy, a few prisoners, forty waggons, and more than a hundred draft-horses, with a considerable booty of cattle and sheep, fell into his hands.

Nor were our operations on General Putnam's right flank less fortunate. To give countenance to the numerous friends of the British government in the county of Monmouth appears to have been a principal motive with Sir William Howe for stretching the chain of his cantonments, by his own confession,* pre-

---

* *Extract of a letter from General Sir* WILLIAM HOWE *to Lord* GEORGE GERMAINE, *dated New-York, December* 20, 1776.
Having mentioned the fruitless attempt of Lord Cornwallis to find boats at Corryel's ferry to pass the Delaware—he proceeds thus:

> The passage of the Delaware being thus rendered impracticable, his Lordship took post at Pennington, in which place and Trenton the two divisions remained until the fourteenth, when the weather having be-

viously to his disaster, rather too far. After that chain became broken, as I have already related, by the blows at Trenton and Princeton, he was obliged to collect, during the rest of the winter, the useless remains in his barracks at Brunswick. In the meantime, General Putnam was much more successful in his attempt to protect our dispersed and dispirited friends in the same district; who, environed on every side by envenomed adversaries, remained inseparably rivetted in affection to American independence. He first detached Colonel Gurney, and afterwards Major Davis,* with such parties of militia as could be spared, for their support. Several skirmishes ensued, in which

---

come too severe to keep the field, and the winter cantonments being arranged, the troops marched from both places to their respective stations. *The chain, I own, is rather too extensive,* but I was induced to occupy Burlington to cover the county of Monmouth, in which there are many loyal inhabitants; and trusting to the almost general submission of the country to the southward of this chain, and to the strength of the corps placed in the advanced posts, I conclude the troops will be in perfect security.

* As there happened to be in my possession a copy of one of his letters to those officers, it was thought worthy of insertion here, in order to demonstrate his satisfaction with their conduct.

To Major JOHN DAVIS, of the third Battalion of Cumberland County Militia.

SIR,

I am much obliged to you for your activity, vigour, and diligence since you have been under my command; you will, therefore, march your men to Philadelphia, and there discharge them; returning into the store all the ammunition, arms and accoutrements you received at that place.

I am, Sir, your humble servant,

ISRAEL PUTNAM.

Princeton, February 5, 1777.

our people had always the advantage. They took, at different times, many prisoners, horses and waggons from foraging parties. In effect, so well did they cover the country, as to induce some of the most respectable inhabitants to declare, that the security of the persons, as well the salvation of the property of many friends to freedom, was owing to the spirited exertions of these two detachments; who, at the same time that they rescued the country from the tyranny of tories, afforded an opportunity for the militia to recover from their consternation, to embody themselves in warlike array, and to stand on their defence.

During this period, General Putnam having received unquestionable intelligence that a party of refugees, in British pay, had taken post, and were erecting a kind of redoubt at Lawrence's Neck, sent Colonel Nelson, with one hundred and fifty militia, to surprise them. That officer conducted with so much secrecy and decision as to take the whole prisoners. These refugees* were commanded by Major Stockton, belonging to Skinner's brigade, and amounted to sixty in number.

A short time after this event Lord Cornwallis sent out another foraging party towards Bound-Brook. General Putnam, having received notice from his emissaries, detached Major Smith, with a few riflemen, to annoy the party, and followed

---

* *Extract of a letter from General* PUTNAM *to the Council of Safety of Pennsylvania, dated at Princeton, February* 18, 1777.

Yesterday evening Colonel Nelson, with a hundred fifty men, at Lawrence's Neck, attacked sixty men of Cortlandt Skinner's Brigade, commanded by the enemy's RENOWNED LAND PILOT *Major Richard Stockton*, routed them, and took the whole prisoners—among them the Major, a Captain and three subalterns, with seventy stand of arms. *Fifty of the Bedford Pennsylvania Riflemen behaved like veterans.*

himself with the rest of his force. Before he could come up, Major Smith, who had formed an ambush, attacked the enemy, killed several horses, took a few prisoners and sixteen baggage-waggons, without sustaining any injury. By such operations, our hero, in the course of the winter, captured nearly a thousand prisoners.

In the latter part of February General Washington advised General Putnam, that, in consequence of a large accession of strength from New-York to the British army at Brunswick, it was to be apprehended they would soon make a forward movement towards the Delaware: in which case the latter was directed to cross the river with his actual force, to assume the command of the militia who might assemble, to secure the boats on the west side of the Delaware, and to facilitate the passage of the rest of the army. But the enemy did not remove from their winter-quarters until the season arrived when green forage could be supplied. In the intermediate period, the correspondence on the part of General Putnam with the Commander in Chief consisted principally of reports and inquiries concerning the treatment of some of the following descriptions of persons: either of those who came within our lines with flags and pretended flags, or who had taken protection from the enemy, or who had been reputed disaffected to our cause, or who were designed to be comprehended in the American Proclamation, which required that those who had taken protections should give them to the nearest American officer, or go within the British lines. The letters of his Excellency in return, generally advisory, were indicative of confidence and approbation.

When the spring had now so far advanced that it was obvious the enemy would soon take the field, the Commander in Chief, after desiring General Putnam to give the officer who was to relieve him at Princeton, all the information necessary for the conduct of that post, appointed that General to the command of a separate army in the Highlands of New-York.

It is scarcely decided, from any documents yet published, whether the preposterous plans prosecuted by the British Generals in the campaign of 1777, were altogether the result of their orders from home, or whether they partially originated from the contingencies of the moment. The system which, at the time, tended to puzzle all human conjecture, when developed, served also to contradict all reasonable calculation. Certain it is, the American Commander in Chief was, for a considerable time, so perplexed with contradictory appearances, that he knew not how to distribute his troops, with his usual discernment, so as to oppose the enemy with equal prospect of success in different parts. The gathering tempests menaced the northern frontiers, the posts in the Highlands, and the city of Philadelphia; but it was still doubtful where the fury of the storm would fall. At one time Sir William Howe was forcing his way by land to Philadelphia; at another, relinquishing the Jerseys; at a third, facing round to make a sudden inroad; then embarking with all the forces that could be spared from New-York; and then putting out to sea, at the very moment when General Burgoyne had reduced Ticonderoga, and seemed to require a co-operation in another quarter.

On our side, we have seen that the old Continental army expired with the year 1776; since which, invention had been tortured with expedients, and zeal with efforts to levy another: for on the success of the recruiting service depended the salvation of the country. The success was such as not to puff us up to presumption, or depress us to despair. The army in the Jerseys, under the orders of the General in Chief, consisted of all the troops raised south of the Hudson; that in the northern department, of the New-Hampshire brigade, two brigades of Massa-

chusetts, and the brigade of New-York, together with some irregular corps; and that in the Highlands, of the remaining two
brigades of Massachusetts, the Connecticut line, consisting of
two brigades, the brigade of Rhode-Island, and one regiment of
New-York. Upon hearing of the loss of Ticonderoga, and the
progress of the British towards Albany, General Washington
ordered the northern army to be reinforced with the two brigades of Massachusetts, then in the Highlands; and, upon finding the army under his immediate command out-numbered by
that of Sir William Howe, which had, by the circuitous route of
the Chesapeak, invaded Pennsylvania, he also called from the
Highlands one of the Connecticut brigades, and that of Rhode-
Island, to his own assistance.

In the neighbourhood of General Putnam there was no enemy capable of exciting alarms. The army left at New-York
seemed only designed for its defence. In it were several entire
corps, composed of tories, who had flocked to the British standard. There was, besides, a band of lurking miscreants, not
properly enrolled, who staid chiefly at West-Chester; from
whence they infested the country between the two armies, pil-
laged the cattle, and carried off the peaceable inhabitants. It was
an unworthy policy in British Generals to patronize banditti.
The whig inhabitants on the edge of our lines, and still lower
down, who had been plundered in a merciless manner, delayed
not to strip the tories in return. People most nearly connected
and allied frequently became most exasperated and inveterate in
malice. Then the ties of fellowship were broken—then friendship itself being soured to enmity, the mind readily gave way to
private revenge, uncontrouled retaliation, and all the deforming
passions that disgrace humanity. Enormities, almost without a
name, were perpetrated, at the description of which, the bosom,
not frozen to apathy, must glow with a mixture of pity and in-

dignation. To prevent the predatory incursions from below, and to cover the county of West-Chester, General Putnam detached from his Head-Quarters, at Peek's-Kill, Meigs's regiment, which, in the course of the campaign, struck several partizan strokes, and achieved the objects for which it was sent. He likewise took measures, without noise or ostentation, to secure himself from being surprised and carried within the British lines by the tories, who had formed a plan for the purpose. The information of this intended enterprise, conveyed to him through several channels, was corroborated by that obtained and transmitted by the Commander in Chief.

It was not wonderful, that many of these tories were able, undiscovered, to penetrate far into the country, and even to go with letters or messages from one British army to another. The inhabitants who were well affected to the royal cause, afforded them every possible support, and their own knowledge of the different routes gave them a farther felicity in performing their peregrinations. Sometimes the most active loyalists, as the tories wished to denominate themselves, who had gone into the British posts, and received promises of commissions upon enlisting a certain number of soldiers, came back again secretly with recruiting instructions. Sometimes these, and others who came from the enemy within the verge of our camps, were detected and condemned to death, in conformity to the usages of war. But the British generals, who had an unlimited supply of money at their command, were able to pay with so much liberality, that emissaries could always be found. Still, it is thought that the intelligence of the American Commanders was, at least, equally accurate; notwithstanding the poverty of their military chest, and the inability of rewarding mercenary agents, for secret services, in proportion to their risk and merit.

A person, by the name of Palmer, who was a lieutenant in the tory new levies, was detected in the camp at Peek's-Kill. Governor Tryon, who commanded the new levies, reclaimed him as a British officer, represented the heinous crime of condemning a man commissioned by his Majesty, and threatened vengeance in case he should be executed. General Putnam wrote the following pithy reply.

> SIR,
>
> Nathan Palmer, a lieutenant in your King's service, was taken in my camp as a *Spy*—he was tried as a *Spy*—he was condemned as a *Spy*—and you may rest assured, Sir, he shall be hanged as a *Spy*.
>
> > I have the honour to be, &c.
> > > ISRAEL PUTNAM.
>
> *His Excellency Governor* TRYON.
> P.S. Afternoon. He is hanged.

Important transactions soon occurred. Not long after the two brigades had marched from Peek's-Kill to Pennsylvania, a reinforcement arrived at New-York from Europe. Appearances indicated that offensive operations would follow. General Putnam having been reduced in force to a single brigade in the field, and a single regiment in garrison at Fort Montgomery, repeatedly informed the Commander in Chief, that the posts committed to his charge must, in all probability, be lost, in case an attempt should be made upon them; and that, circumstanced as he was, he could not be responsible for the consequences. His situation was certainly to be lamented; but it was not in the power of the Commander in Chief to alter it, except by authorising him to call upon the militia for aid—an aid always precarious, and often so tardy, as, when obtained, to be of no utility.

On the fifth of October Sir Henry Clinton came up the North-River with three thousand men. After making many feints to mislead the attention, he landed, the next morning, at Stony-Point, and commenced his march over the mountains to Fort Montgomery. Governor Clinton, an active, resolute, and intelligent officer, who commanded the garrison, upon being apprised of the movement, dispatched a letter, by express, to General Putnam for succour. By the treachery of the messenger, the letter miscarried. General Putnam, astonished at hearing nothing respecting the enemy, rode, with General Parsons, and Colonel Root, his Adjutant-General, to reconnoitre them at King's Ferry. In the meantime, at five o'clock in the afternoon, Sir Henry Clinton's columns, having surmounted the obstacles and barriers of nature, descended from the Thunder-Hill, through thickets impassible but for light troops, and* attacked

---

* The author of these Memoirs, then Major of Brigade to the first Connecticut brigade, was alone at Head-Quarters when the firing began. He hastened to Colonel Wyllys, the senior officer in camp, and advised him to dispatch all the men not on duty to Fort Montgomery, without waiting for orders. About five hundred men marched instantly under Colonel Meigs; and the author, with Dr. Beardsley, a surgeon in the brigade, rode, at full speed, through a bye-path, to let the garrison know, that a reinforcement was on its march. Notwithstanding all the haste these officers made to and over the river, the fort was so completely invested on their arrival, that it was impossible to enter. They went on board the new frigate which lay near the fortress, and had the misfortune to be idle, though not unconcerned spectators of the storm. They saw the minutest actions distinctly when the works were carried. The frigate, after receiving several platoons, slipped her cable, and proceeded a little way up the river; but the wind and tide becoming adverse, the crew set her on fire, to prevent her falling into the hands of the enemy, whose ships were approaching. The louring darkness of the night, the profound stillness that reigned, the interrupted flashes of the flames that illuminated the waters, the

the different redoubts. The garrison, inspired by the conduct of their leaders, defended the works with distinguished valour. But, as the post had been designed principally to prevent the passing of ships, and as an assault in rear had not been expected, the works on the land side were incomplete and untenable. In the dusk of twilight, the British entered with their bayonets fixed. Their loss was inconsiderable. Nor was that of the garrison great. Governor Clinton, his brother General James Clinton, Colonel Dubois, and most of the officers and men effected their escape under cover of the thick smoke and darkness that suddenly prevailed. The capture of this fort by Sir Henry Clinton, together with the consequent removal of the chains and booms that obstructed the navigation, opened a passage to Albany, and seemed to favour a junction of his force with that of General Burgoyne. But the latter having been compelled to capitulate a few days after this event, and great numbers of militia having arrived from New-England, the successful army returned to New-York; yet not before a detachment from it, under the orders of General Vaughan, had burnt the defenceless town of Esopus, and several scattering buildings on the banks of the river.

Notwithstanding the army in the Highlands had been so much weakened, for the sake of strengthening the armies in other quarters, as to have occasioned the loss of Fort Montgomery, yet that loss was productive of no consequences. Our main army in Pennsylvania, after having contended with supe-

---

long shadows of the cliffs that now and then were seen, the explosion of the cannon which were left loaded in the ship, and the reverberating echo which resounded, at intervals, between the stupendous mountains on both sides of the river, composed an awful night-piece for persons prepared by the preceding scene, to contemplate subjects of horrid sublimity.

rior force in two indecisive battles, still held the enemy in check; while the splendid success which attended our arms at the northward, gave a more favourable aspect to the American affairs, at the close of this campaign, than they had ever before assumed.

When the enemy fell back to New-York by water, we followed them a part of the way by land. Colonel Meigs, with a detachment from the several regiments in General Parsons's brigade, having made a forced march from Crompond to West-Chester, surprised and broke up for a time the band of free-booters, of whom he brought off fifty, together with many cattle and horses which they had recently stolen.

Soon after this enterprise General Putnam advanced towards the British lines. As he had received intelligence that small bodies of the enemy were out, with orders from Governor Tryon to burn Wright's mills, he prevented it by detaching three parties, of one hundred men in each. One of these parties fell in with and captured thirty-five, and another forty of the new levies. But as he could not prevent a third hostile party from burning the house of Mr. Van Tassel, a noted whig and a committee-man, who was forced to go along with them, naked and barefoot, on the icy ground, in a freezing night, he, for the professed purpose of retaliation, sent Captain Buchanan, in a whale-boat, to burn the house of General Oliver Delancey on York Island. Buchanan effected his object, and by this expedition put a period, for the present, to that unmeaning and wanton species of destruction.

While General Putnam quartered at New-Rochelle, a scouting party, which had been sent to West-Farms, below West-Chester, surrounded the house in which Colonel James Delancey lodged, and, notwithstanding he crept under the bed the better to be concealed, brought him to Head-Quarters before morning.

This officer was exchanged by the British General without delay, and placed at the head of the cow-boys, a licentious corps of irregulars, who, in the sequel, committed unheard-of depredations and excesses.

It was distressing to see so beautiful a part of the country so barbarously wasted, and often to witness some peculiar scene of female misery: for most of the female inhabitants had been obliged to fly within the lines possessed by one army or the other. Near our quarters was an affecting instance of human vicissitude. Mr. William Sutton, of Maroneck, an inoffensive man, a merchant by profession, who lived in a decent fashion, and whose family had as happy prospects as almost any in the country, upon some imputation of toryism, went to the enemy. His wife, oppressed with grief in the disagreeable state of dereliction, did not long survive. Betsey Sutton, their eldest daughter, was a modest and lovely young woman, of about fifteen years old, when, at the death of her mother, the care of five or six younger children devolved upon her. She was discreet and provident beyond her years; but when we saw her, she looked to be feeble in health—broken in spirit—wan, melancholy, and dejected. She said that "their last cow, which furnished milk for the children, had lately been taken away—that they had frequently been plundered of their wearing apparel and furniture, she believed by both parties—that they had little more to lose—and that she knew not where to procure bread for the dear little ones, who had no father to provide for them"—*no mother*—she was going to have said—but a torrent of tears choked articulation. In coming to that part of the country again, after some campaigns had elapsed, I found the habitation desolate, and the garden overgrown with weeds. Upon inquiry, I learnt, that as soon as we left the place, some ruffians broke into the house while she lay in bed, in the latter part of the night; and that, having been terrified by their rudeness, she ran, half-naked, into a neighbouring swamp, where she continued until the morning—there the poor girl caught a violent cold, which ended in a consumption. It finished a life without a spot—and a career of sufferings commenced and continued without a fault.

Sights of wretchedness always touched with commiseration the feelings of General Putnam, and prompted his generous soul to succour the afflicted. But the indulgence which he showed, whenever it did not militate against his duty, towards the deserted and suffering families of the tories in the State of New-York, was the cause of his becoming unpopular with no inconsiderable class of people in that State. On the other side, he had conceived an unconquerable aversion to many of the persons who were entrusted with the disposal of tory-property, because he believed them to have been guilty of peculations and other infamous practices. But although the enmity between him and the sequestrators was acrimonious as mutual, yet he lived in habits of amity with the most respectable characters in public departments, as well as in private life.

His character was also respected by the enemy. He had been acquainted with many of the principal officers in a former war. As flags frequently passed between the out-posts, during his continuance on the lines, it was a common practice to forward newspapers by them; and as those printed by Rivington, the royal printer in New-York, were infamous for the falsehoods with which they abounded, General Putnam once sent a packet to his old friend General Robertson, with this billet:

Major-General Putnam presents his compliments to Major-General Robertson, and sends him some American newspapers for his perusal—when General Robertson shall have done with them, it is requested they be given to Rivington, in order that he may print some truth.

Late in the year we left the lines and repaired to the Highlands; for upon the loss of Fort Montgomery, the Commander in Chief determined to build another fortification for the defence of the river. His Excellency, accordingly, wrote to General Putnam to fix upon the spot. After reconnoitering all the different places proposed, and revolving in his own mind their relative advantages for offence on the water and defence on the land, he fixed upon WEST-POINT. It is no vulgar praise to say, that to him belongs the glory of having chosen this rock of our military salvation. The position for water-batteries, which might sweep the channel where the river formed a right angle, made it the most proper of any for commanding the navigation; while the rocky ridges that rose in awful sublimity behind each other, rendered it impregnable, and even incapable of being invested by less than twenty thousand men. The British, who considered this post as a sort of American Gibraltar, never attempted it but by the treachery of an American officer. All the world knows that this project failed, and that West-Point continues to be the receptacle of every thing valuable in military preparations to the present day.

In the month of January, 1778, when a snow, two feet deep, lay on the earth, General Parsons's brigade went to West-Point and broke ground. Want of covering for the troops, together with want of tools and materials for the works, made the prospect truly gloomy and discouraging. It was necessary that means should be found, though our currency was depreciated and our treasury exhausted. The estimates and requisitions of Colonel la Radiere, the engineer who laid out the works, altogether disproportioned to our circumstances, served only to put us in mind of our poverty, and, as it were, to satirize our resources. His petulant behaviour and unaccommodating disposition added further embarrassments. It was then that the patriotism of Governor Clinton shone in full lustre. His exertions to furnish supplies can never be too much commended. His influence, arising from his popularity, was unlimited: yet he hesitated not to put all his popularity at risk, whenever the federal interests demanded. Notwithstanding the impediments that opposed our progress, with his aid, before the opening of the campaign, the works were in great forwardness.

According to a resolution of Congress, an inquiry was to be made into the causes of military disasters. Major-General M'Dougall, Brigadier-General Huntington, and Colonel Wigglesworth composed the Court of Inquiry on the loss of Fort Montgomery. Upon full knowledge and mature deliberation of facts, on the spot, they reported the loss to have been occasioned by want of men, and not by any fault in the Commanders.

General Putnam, who during the investigation was relieved from duty, as soon as Congress had approved the report, took command of the right wing of the grand army, under the orders of the General in Chief. This was just after the battle of Monmouth, when the three armies which had last year acted separately, joined at the White-Plains. Our effective force, in one camp, was at no other time so respectable as at this juncture. The army consisted of sixty regular regiments of foot, formed into fifteen brigades, four battalions of artillery, four regiments of horse, and several corps of State troops. But as the enemy kept close within their lines on York Island, nothing could be attempted. Towards the end of autumn we broke up the camp, and went first to Fredericksburgh, and thence to winter-quarters.

In order to cover the country adjoining to the *Sound*, and to support the garrison of *West-Point*, in case of an attack, Major-

General Putnam was stationed for the winter at Reading, in Connecticut. He had under his orders the brigade of New-Hampshire, the two brigades of Connecticut, the corps of infantry commanded by Hazen, and that of cavalry by Sheldon.

The troops, who had been badly fed, badly cloathed, and worse paid, by brooding over their grievances in the leisure and inactivity of winter-quarters, began to think them intolerable. The Connecticut brigades formed the design of marching to Hartford, where the General Assembly was then in session, and of demanding redress at the point of the bayonet. Word having been brought to General Putnam, that the second brigade was under arms for this purpose, he mounted his horse, gallopped to the cantonment, and thus addressed them:

My brave lads, whither are you going? Do you intend to desert your officers, and to invite the enemy to follow you into the country? Whose cause have you been fighting and suffering so long in—is it not your own? Have you no property, no parents, wives or children. You have behaved like men so far—all the world is full of your praises—and posterity will stand astonished at your deeds: but not if you spoil all at last. Don't you consider how much the country is distressed by the war, and that your officers have not been any better paid than yourselves? But we all expect better times, and that the country, will do us ample justice. Let us all stand by one another, then, and fight it out like brave soldiers. Think what a shame it would be for Connecticut men to run away from their officers.

After the several regiments had received the General as he rode along the line *with drums beating, and presented arms,* the sergeants who had then the command, brought the men *to an order,* in which position they continued while he was speaking. When he had done, he directed the acting Major of Brigade to give the word for them to shoulder, march to their regimental parades, and lodge arms; all which they executed with promptitude and apparent good humour. One soldier only, who had been the most active, was confined in the quarter-guard; from whence, at night, he attempted to make his escape. But the sentinel, who had also been in the mutiny, shot him dead on the spot, and thus the affair subsided.

About the middle of winter, while General Putnam was on visit to his out-post at Horse-Neck, he found Governor Tryon advancing upon that town with a corps of fifteen hundred men. To oppose these General Putnam had only a picquet of one hundred and fifty men, and two iron field-pieces, without horses or dragropes. He, however, planted his cannon on the high ground, by the meeting-house, and retarded their approach by firing several times, until, perceiving the horse (supported by the infantry) about to charge, he ordered the picquet to provide for their safety, by retiring to a swamp inaccessible to horse, and secured his own, by plunging down the steep precipice at the church upon a full trot. This precipice is so steep, where he descended, as to have artificial stairs, composed of nearly one hundred stone steps, for the accommodation of foot passengers. There the Dragoons, who were but a sword's length from him, stopped short; for the declivity was so abrupt, that they ventured not to follow; and, before they could gain the valley, by going round the brow of the hill in the ordinary road, he was far enough beyond their reach. He continued his route, unmolested, to Stanford; from whence, having strengthened his picquet by the junction of some militia, he came back again, and, in turn, pursued Governor Tryon in his retreat. As he rode down the precipice, one ball, of the many fired at him, went through his beaver: But Governor Tryon, by way of compensation for spoiling his hat, sent him, soon afterwards, as a present, a complete suit of clothes.

In the campaign of 1779, which terminated the career of General Putnam's services, he commanded the Maryland line, posted at Butter-milk falls, about two miles below West-Point. He was happy in possessing the friendship of the officers of that line, and in living on terms of hospitality with them. Indeed, there was no family in the army that lived better than his own. The General, his second son Major Daniel Putnam, and the writer of these memoirs, composed that family. This campaign, principally spent in strengthening the works of West-Point, was only signalised for the storm of Stony-Point by the light-infantry under the conduct of General Wayne, and the surprise of the post of Powles-Hook by the corps under the command of Colonel Henry Lee. When the army quitted the field, and marched to Morris-Town, into winter-quarters, General Putnam's family went into Connecticut for a few weeks. In December the General began his journey to Morris-Town. Upon the road between Pomfret and Hartford he felt an unusual torpor slowly pervading his right hand and foot. This heaviness crept gradually on, and until it had deprived him of the use of his limbs on that side, in a considerable degree, before he reached the house of his friend Colonel Wadsworth. Still he was unwilling to consider his disorder of the paralytic kind, and endeavoured to shake it off by exertion. Having found that impossible, a temporary dejection, disguised, however, under a veil of assumed cheerfulness, succeeded. But reason, philosophy, and religion, soon reconciled him to his fate. In that situation he has constantly remained, favoured with such a portion of bodily activity as enables him to walk and ride moderately; and retaining, unimpaired, his relish for enjoyment, his love of pleasantry, his strength of memory, and all the faculties of his mind. As a proof that the powers of memory are not weakened, it ought to be observed, that he has lately repeated, from recollection, all the adventures of his life, which are here recorded, and which had formerly been communicated to the compiler in detached conversations.

In patient, yet fearless expectation of the approach of THE KING OF TERRORS, whom he hath full often faced in the field of blood, the Christian hero now enjoys, in domestic retirement, the fruit of his early industry. Having in youth provided a competent subsistence for old age, he was secured from the danger of penury and distress, to which so many officers and soldiers, worn out in the public service, have been reduced. To illustrate his merits the more fully, this Essay will be concluded with a copy of the last letter written to him, by General Washington, in his military character.

Head-Quarters, 2d June, 1783.

DEAR SIR,

Your favour of the 20th of May I received with much pleasure. For I can assure you that among the many worthy and meritorious officers with whom I have had the happiness to be connected in service through the course of this war, and from whose cheerful assistance in the various trying vicissitudes of a complicated contest, *the name of a* PUTNAM *is not forgotten;* nor will be but with that stroke of time which shall obliterate from my mind the remembrance of all those toils and fatigues through which we have struggled for the preservation and establishment of the *Rights, Liberties,* and *Independence* of our *Country.*

Your congratulations on the happy prospects of peace and independent security, with their attendant blessings to the UNITED STATES, I receive with great satisfaction; and beg that you will accept a return of my gratulations to you on this auspicious event—an event, in which, great as it is in itself, and glorious as it will probably be in its consequences, you have a right to participate largely, from the distinguished part you have contributed towards its attainment.

But while I contemplate the greatness of the object for which we have contended, and felicitate you on the happy issue of our toils and labours, which have terminated with such general satisfaction, I lament that you should feel the ungrateful returns of a country, in whose service you have exhausted your bodily strength, and expended the vigour of a youthful constitution. I wish, however, that your expectations of returning liberality may be verified. I have a hope they may—but should they not, your case will not be a singular one. *Ingratitude has been experienced in all ages, and* REPUBLICS, *in particular, have ever been famed for the exercise of that unnatural and* SORDID VICE.

The SECRETARY AT WAR, who is now here, informs me that you have ever been considered as entitled to full pay since your absence from the field, and that you will still be considered in that light until the close of the war; at which period you will be equally entitled to the same emoluments of half-pay or commutation as other officers of your rank. The same opinion is also given by the Pay-Master-General, who is now with the army, impowered by Mr. Morris for the settlement of all their accounts, and who will attend to yours whenever you shall think proper to send on for the purpose, which it will probably be best for you to do in a short time.

I anticipate, with pleasure, the day, and that, I trust, not far off, when I shall quit the busy scenes of a military employment, and retire to the more tranquil walks of domestic life. In that, or whatever other situation Providence may dispose of my future days, THE REMEMBRANCE OF

THE MANY FRIENDSHIPS AND CONNECTIONS I HAVE HAD THE HAPPINESS TO CONTRACT WITH THE GEN-TLEMEN OF THE ARMY, WILL BE ONE OF MY MOST GRATEFUL REFLECTIONS. *Under this contemplation, and impressed with the sentiments of benevolence and regard, I commend you, my dear Sir, my other friends, and with them, the interests and happiness of our dear country, to the* KEEP-ING AND PROTECTION OF ALMIGHTY GOD.

I have the honour to be, &c.

GEORGE WASHINGTON.

To the honourable Major-General PUTNAM.

GENERAL PUTNAM died the 29th of May, 1790.

An Oration on the Political Situation of the
United States of America in the Year 1789

Pronounced before the State Society of the
Cincinnati of Connecticut, at New-Haven, in Celebration
of the Thirteenth Anniversary of Independence
Published at the Request of the Society

Since the last Anniversary of Independence, my dear
fellow-citizens, we have been witnesses to the complete
establishment of a new general government. On an event
of such magnitude, the voice of congratulation has already been
heard from one extreme of our land to the other. But as our fe-
licitations can never be more grateful than at the time when we
are convened to commemorate the birth of our nation, it may,
perhaps, be expected, from the task I am called upon to perform
this day, that I should be the organ for expressing the part we
bear in this universal joy. I feel a confidence, from the sensations
of my own heart, that every bosom in this assembly beats high
at the thought of our country's happiness. Even the ardent eyes
and the animated countenances of all who compose it, attest
how sincerely they rejoice in the prospect before them. But, in
the midst of our rejoicings, we ought to remember, that no occasion can be more suitable than the present for employing our
reflections on our political situation. I will therefore hope for
your indulgence, while I make a few observations on the Amer-

ican revolution; on the necessity which afterwards appeared for establishing a general government of more energy than the original confederation; on the nature of the government which has lately been carried into effect; and on the national prosperity which we may reasonably expect will result from the faithful administration of that government.

At the commencement of the late war with Great-Britain, when we thought ourselves justifiable in resisting to blood, it was known to those best acquainted with the different conditions of the combatants, and the probable cost of the prize in dispute, that the expense, in comparison with our circumstances as colonists, must be enormous—the struggle protracted, doubtful, and severe. It was known that the resources of Britain were almost inexhaustible, that her fleets covered the ocean, and that her troops had harvested laurels in every quarter of the globe. Not then organized as a nation, or known as a people on the earth, we had no preparations. Money, the nerve of war, was wanting. The sword was to be forged on the anvil of necessity; the treasury to be created from nothing. If we had a resource, unknown to our enemy, it was in the unconquerable resolution of our citizens, the conscious rectitude of our cause, and a confident trust that we should not be forsaken by heaven. The people willingly offered themselves to the battle; but the means of arming, clothing and subsisting them, as well as of providing the general implements of hostility, were only to be found in anticipations of our future wealth. Bills of credit were emitted; monies borrowed for the most pressing emergencies; and our men in the field unpaid for their services. At this time the magnanimous monarch of France reached a fostering hand to assist in rescuing us from ruin. In this manner, peace, attended with every circumstance that could gratify our reasonable desires, was at length obtained; but a load of debt was left upon us. The fluctuation of our paper currency, and the consequent frequency of speculation in it, had, in too many instances, occasioned vague ideas of property, produced licentious appetites, and corrupted the morals of men. To these immediate consequences of a fluctuating medium of commerce, may be joined a tide of circumstances, that flowed together from sources mostly opened during and after the war. The ravage of farms, the conflagration of towns, the diminution of agriculture, the extinction of trade, the embarrassment of some who were indebted to British merchants before the war, the privation in all, during its continuance, of many conveniences of life, the subsequent influx of merchandize, the tempting facility of procuring it without present payment, the growing taste for extravagance, and the habit, too soon acquired, of deferring or eluding satisfaction for just obligations, now began to overwhelm the continent with private distress, bankruptcy, and breach of faith.

From this period also our public affairs were seen to decline. I will ask your attention for a moment, while I speak of the unsatisfactory part of our old confederation, and the necessity that became apparent for instituting a different form of government. It is not a subject of wonder that the first project of a federal government, formed on the defective models of some foreign confederacies, in the midst of a war, before we had much experience in political affairs, and while, from the concurrence of external danger, and the patriotic impulse of the moment, implicit obedience was yielded to the requisitions of an advisory council, should have been imperfect. Our astonishment ought rather to be excited, that, feeble and inefficient as the government was, it not only carried us in safety through the war, but kept us from severance until another could be substituted. By the original confederation, the right to make demands on the several States for such pecuniary supplies as might be necessary for defraying the expenses of the war, and for supporting the government of the union, together with some other specific prerogatives of sovereignty, were committed to Congress. But Congress, constituted in most respects as a diplomatic body, possessed no power of carrying into execution a single resolution, however urgently dictated by prudence, policy or justice. The individual communities, knowing there existed no power of coercion, treated with neglect, whenever it suited their convenience or caprice, the most salutary measures and the most indispensable requisitions of Congress. Experience taught us, that the powers given by the members of the union to their federal head, were not sufficient to enable it to accomplish the purposes for which the body politic had been formed. We now touched on the hour of humiliation. The confederacy was found to be a government in name rather than in reality. Hence the interest due on our public debts remained unpaid. Hence many a veteran was reduced to unmerited distress. Hence we were continually liable, on our own part, to have infractions made upon treaties, which were equally honourable, advantageous and sacred. Hence we were in danger of having our faith become as proverbial as that of Carthage, and our name the scorn of the earth. Hence there was a nation, which, in some measure, excluded our vessels from its ports, burdened our commerce with intolerable impositions, introduced its ships into our carrying trade, and, because we were destitute of a retaliating power, refused to enter into a commercial treaty with us. With a debt accumulating from the necessity of obtaining repeated loans; with a credit much impaired for the want of punctuality, and apprehension of national bankruptcy; with cries for justice from the widow, the fatherless, and the soldier worn out in his country's defence, ascending to that Being who hath purer eyes than to behold iniquity with impunity, who is a God of vengeance, as well as a

God of justice—whither could we turn for succour? where could we fly for refuge?

The veil that concealed this melancholy and afflicting picture was at last withdrawn. The wise and the good stood astonished at the sight; none but the ignorant or the wicked rested unconcerned. Even fearfulness seized, in many instances, upon those well-meaning politicians whose security had been produced by the scantiness of their information, and the confinement of their views to the local advantages of the States to which they belonged. Then it was that men, better informed and more conversant in civil affairs, began to dread that a free, yet efficient government, the object which animated in life, and soothed in death, those heroes who had sealed their principles with their blood, must still be lost: that the prospect of national happiness, which invigorated our arms and cheered our hearts through the perilous struggle for independence, must vanish for ever from our view: and that the hope of establishing the empire of reason, justice, philosophy, and religion, throughout the extensive regions of the new world, would be considered but the illusion of a heated imagination. And what could be more mortifying to every true patriot, than to perceive our countrymen ready to rush headlong on their ruin—ready to destroy the asylum which was just offered for suffering humanity—ready to verify the predictions of our foes, that our independence would prove a curse to its votaries—and, by frustrating the fairest opportunity ever afforded for a people to become great and happy in the enjoyment of freedom, to confirm the detestable doctrine, that mankind, unequal to the task of governing themselves, were made for a state of slavery?—Thus our old confederation seemed passing away. Our day of political probation appeared expiring. The *Republic* was about to assume, if I may be allowed the expression, a renovated body, prepared for a more permanent state of existence in bliss or woe. Life and death were in our option. The first was involved in UNION under a good general government—the last in SEPARATION into a number of miserable fragments of empire. So long as strength must be deemed preferable to weakness, harmony to confusion, peace to war, happiness to misery, and independence to subjugation, the American people, who will always judge right when they shall have the means of information, could not hesitate to prefer the former. Nor is it unworthy of remark, that, amidst the variety of opinions which prevailed respecting the system of government proper to be adopted, no man was found so hardy as to outrage the feelings of his countrymen, by openly advocating counsels of disunion. And may we not, uninfluenced by superstition, believe that heaven infused the idea into our legislatures, to convoke a national assembly, at this interesting and awful crisis!

The result is so well known, that I forbear to dilate upon it. Happily the spirit of accommodation, that influenced the Convention, has been diffused among their countrymen. The adoption of the government by so many communities, distinct in their views and interests, will be an immortal memorial of victory gained by enlightened reason over brutal force. Can we contemplate a whole people, like a nation of philosophers, discussing and agreeing on a form of government: can we contemplate a work so vast in its import, and so wonderfully effected—not by violence and bloodshed, but by deliberation and consent—without exclaiming in rapturous admiration, behold a new thing under the sun! and without uttering in grateful adoration, lo, this is indeed the LORD's doing, and it is marvellous in our eyes!

Without presuming to trespass on your patience so far as to attempt to analyze the Constitution, or to demonstrate its merits by logical deductions, I may, perhaps, be permitted just to observe, that it appears to be, in its formation, a government of the people, that is to say, a government in which all power is derived from, and, at stated periods, reverts to them—and that, in its operation, it is a government of laws made and executed by the fair substitutes of the people alone. The election of the different branches of Congress by the freemen, either directly or indirectly, is the pivot on which turns the first wheel of government—a wheel which communicates motion to the whole machine: at the same time, the exercise of this right of election seems to be so regulated, as to afford less opportunity for corruption and influence, and more for stability and volition, than has usually been incident to popular governments. Nor could the members of Congress exempt themselves from the consequences of any unjust or tyrannical acts which they might impose upon others: for, in a short time, they will mingle with the mass of the people. Their interests must therefore be the same, and their feelings in sympathy with those of their constituents. Besides, their re-election must always depend upon the good reputation which they shall have maintained in the judgment of their fellow citizens. Hence we may be induced to conclude, that this government is less obnoxious to well-founded objections than most which have existed in the world. And in that opinion we may be confirmed on three accounts: *First,* because every government ought to be possessed of powers adequate to the purposes for which it was instituted; *secondly,* because no other, or greater powers, appear to be delegated to this government, than are essential to attain the objects for which it was instituted, to wit, the safety and happiness of the governed; and, *thirdly,* because it is clear, that no government, before introduced among mankind, ever contained so many checks, or such efficacious restraints, to prevent it from degenerating into any species of oppression. It is unnecessary to be insisted upon, because it is well understood, that the impotence of Congress under the former confederation, and the inexpediency of trusting sufficiently ample prerogatives to a single body, gave birth to the different branches which constitute the present general government. Convinced that the balances, arising from the distribution of the Legislative, Executive, and Judicial powers in this government, are the best which have hitherto been instituted, I presume not to assert that better may not still be devised. To avoid a wanton levity of innovation on the one hand, and an unalterable practice of error on the other, are points in policy equally desirable, though, I believe, a constitutional power to effect them never before existed. Whether the mode which is pointed out in this Constitution, for procuring amendments, be not the wisest, and apparently the happiest expedient that ever has been suggested by human prudence, I leave every unprejudiced mind to determine. If, in the mean time, it was a given point, that the late federal government could not have existed much longer; if, without some speedy remedy, a dissolution of the union must have ensued; if, without adhering to the union, we could have no security against falling a prey to foreign invasion or domestic usurpation; if upon our adherence to the union depended the protection of our property at home, and the profits of our commerce abroad; if the almost unanimous agreement of the federal Convention upon this plan of government, under the local prejudices and various expectations of the States, could be deemed little short of miraculous; if there was an easy provision made for the correction of such errors as should be found, from the imbecility of human nature, to have insinuated themselves into it; and if, upon a rejection previous to amendments, there did not appear any probability that the same system could be soon enough amended, or any other substituted in its place

by another Convention—surely no State* ought to have re-
jected it without pondering well on the consequences: because,
anarchy and civil war, with an eventual government of chance
or force, appeared but too probable consequences of a general
rejection.

Under such circumstances it was doubtless the part of wisdom to adopt the Constitution. I pretend to no unusual fore-
sight into futurity, and therefore cannot undertake to decide
what may be its ultimate fate. If a promised good should terminate in an unexpected evil, it would not be a solitary example
of disappointment. If the blessings of heaven, showered thick
around us, should be spilled on the ground, or converted to
curses through the fault of those for whose use they were prof-
fered, it would not be the first instance of folly or perverseness
in short-sighted mortals. The blessed religion, revealed in the
word of God, will remain an eternal and awful monument to
prove, that the best institutions may be abused by human de-
pravity; and that they may even, in some instances, be made
subservient to the vilest of purposes. Should, hereafter, those
who are intrusted with the management of this government, in-
cited by the lust of domination, and prompted by the supine-
ness or venality of their constituents, break down the barriers of
this Constitution, and trample on the prostrated rights of humanity, it will only serve to show that no compact among men,
however provident in its construction, and sacred in its ratifi-
cation, can be pronounced everlasting and inviolable; and, if I
may so express myself, that no wall of words, that no mound of
parchment, can be so formed as to stand against the sweeping

---

*At this time, the States of North-Carolina and Rhode-Island had not ac-
ceded to the general government.

135

torrent of boundless ambition on the one side, aided by the sapping current of corrupted morals on the other. But until the people of America shall have lost all virtue; until they shall have become totally insensible to the differences between liberty and slavery; until they shall have been reduced to such poverty of spirit as to be willing to sell that pre-eminent blessing of rational beings, the *birth-right of freedom;* in short, until they shall have been found incapable of governing themselves, and ripe for a master, these consequences, I should fondly hope, can never arrive.

I proceed now, in the order proposed, to treat of the head that was reserved for the conclusion of this discourse: I mean the national prosperity which we may reasonably expect will result from the faithful administration of this government. My chief design in mentioning a few circumstances eminently calculated to promote our happiness as a people, is to increase a disposition to make the best possible use of those circumstances. Can there be any pursuit more consonant to the dictates of reason and nature, than that whose object is the promotion of the happiness of our country? To embrace this object in its utmost limit, our imaginations must expand with the dimensions of a continent, and extend with the revolutions of futurity.

The preliminary observation, that a free government ought to be founded on the information and morals of the people, will here find its proper place. Happily our citizens are remarkably instructed by education, docile to duty, and ingenious for making improvements. More knowledge is, perhaps, at this moment diffused among them, than among any other people under heaven. The conduct and issue of the late war may be a criterion to decide, whether they are destitute of wisdom in the cabinet, or fortitude in the field. For investigation of the rights of man, for ingenuity in applying principles already discovered

to works of mechanism, for inventions in useful arts, and for re-
searches in several branches of philosophy, few have gone before
them. Even for efforts of genius, in some of the finer arts, they
are thought, by the best judges, scarcely to have been excelled in
the present age. The world has applauded their public writings,
for the good sense and manly diction by which they are distinguished. Yet it is not for us, who claim no more than to be upon
a level with our fellow-men, to encourage one another in entertaining too high an opinion of ourselves. It is enough that we
do not feel a degrading consciousness of belonging to that in-
ferior class of mortals, in which some of the philosophers of
Europe have had the presumption to place us. On the contrary,
peculiar fields of nature and contemplation are peculiarly favourable to the expansion of the human powers. If we possess
any grandeur of soul, any penetration of thought, any combination for project, the great scenes of nature with which we are
surrounded, and the great political drama in which we are required to take a part, will call them into action. When we reflect
upon our relative situation, we cannot consider ourselves as
members of a petty community, or as beings acting for a fleeting
moment. We are not, like many of the European States, limited
to our present numbers. Though it should be the primary object
of our rulers to promote the immediate felicity of a nation, as
singular in its origin as new to political life; yet they cannot forget, that the happiness of countless millions, who are to draw
their first breath in America, may depend, in a great degree, on
the discipline, institutions, and examples of this generation. For
certain it is, the population of our country must increase almost
beyond the power of calculation. The stream of people, wave
propelling wave, must, with the lapse of years, roll back to the
Lake of the Woods. From our geographical position, it is not
for kings and parliaments, with their assumed omnipotence, to

stop those waves in their proper course. It is not for impolitic princes, vainly checking our commerce for momentary gain, to prevent us from becoming a commercial, a rich, and a powerful people. Had they really a design of accomplishing this, it would be adviseable to begin with annihilating our natural advantages, with drying up our innumerable navigable rivers, and with sterilizing the uncommon fertility of our soil.

The benign effects which, in all human probability, will be produced by the faithful administration of this government, must not be entirely passed in silence, though they can be but imperfectly noticed. Hitherto, for want of an efficient government, the felicities that were promised by our situation, and the advantages that were expected from our independence, have not equalled our hopes. The harvest of blessings, sown in fields fattened with the blood of heroes, hath mocked our expectations. But under the present Constitution, being uncommonly protected in our persons and our acquisitions, we shall have uncommonly favourable opportunities for increasing and enjoying our natural resources. We have purchased wisdom by experience. Though mankind are believed to be averse to the coercions of government, yet no sooner had our countrymen felt the inconveniencies arising from the feebleness of our former confederation, than they seemed willing to invest a new Congress with a farther portion of their original rights, for the purpose of being more fully protected in the enjoyment of the remainder. Thus the dispositions of our countrymen have been gradually matured to receive an energetic government. Heaven be thanked that we have lived to see its wonders in our native land, not less in darkness and tempest than in sunshine and serenity! Now the clouds that obscured our political horizon are bursting away. The dawn of happiness begins to appear. We cannot refrain from experiencing the consolatory joys of futurity, in contemplating the immense deserts, yet untrodden by the foot of man, soon to become fair as the garden of God, soon to be animated by the activity of multitudes, and soon to be made vocal with the praises of the MOST HIGH. Can it be imagined that so many peculiar advantages of soil and of climate, for agriculture, for navigation, and eventually for manufactures, were lavished in vain—or that this vast continent was not created and reserved so long undiscovered, as a theatre for those glorious displays of Divine power and goodness, the salutary consequences of which will flow to another hemisphere, and extend through the interminable series of ages! Should not our souls exult in the prospect? Though we shall not survive to perceive, with these bodily senses, but a small portion of the blessed effects which our revolution will occasion in the rest of the world; yet we may enjoy the progress of human society, and human happiness, in anticipation. We may rejoice in a belief, that intellectual light will yet illuminate the dark corners of the earth; that freedom of inquiry will produce liberality of conduct; that mankind will reverse the absurd position, that the *many* were made for the *few;* and that they will not continue slaves in one quarter of the globe, when they can become freemen in another.

With such animating prospects before us; with a spirit of industry becoming every day more prevalent; with habits of economy, first prompted by necessity, now acquiring force from fashion; with dispositions that a reverence for public and private justice should form the basis of our national character; we only wanted a good government, well administered, to establish our happiness at home, and our respectability abroad. This is the time for fixing our national character and national manners. For this purpose, the integrity, the talents, and the examples of such an assemblage of illustrious personages as those who are now employed in the general government, were highly requisite.

Notwithstanding the unanimous suffrage of our countrymen in favour of the Supreme Magistrate supersedes the propriety of my mentioning the circumstances of his coming again into public life, the sentiments entertained of his character, and the benefits expected from his administration; yet I may be allowed to say, that no selection of sages, in this or any other country, ever merited the confidence of their fellow-citizens more than the members of the present Congress. If then the body of worthy citizens will cooperate with the general and state governments, in endeavours to promote the public felicity; if the ministers of religion will exert themselves in their holy functions to disseminate peace and goodwill among men; if the executive officers of government will not bear the sword of justice in vain, but be a terror to evil doers and a praise to such as shall do well; we may congratulate ourselves upon having lived at so important a period, and seen the establishment of a government calculated to promote the permanent prosperity and glory of our nation.

Index

Abercrombie, General James, 31; at Ticonderoga, 36
Adams, John and Abigail, xv
Albany, New York, 115
Albemarle, George Keppel, Lord, 56
Alner, Captain James, 80n
American Turtle (submarine machine), 82–87
Amherst, General Jeffrey, 39; Detroit campaign of, 58; Montreal campaign of, 53–55
Assemblies, Provincial: on Stamp Act, 59, 62

Barlow, Joel: *The Vision of Columbus*, x, 8n, 73–74
The Battle of the Kegs (Hopkinson), 83n–87n
Bedford Pennsylvania Riflemen, 108
Biography: Plutarchan, xiii, xvii; purpose of, 5–6
Boston: British possession of, 74; Washington's occupation of, 77
Boston Port Bill, 63
Bound-Brook, New Jersey: foraging at, 108

Bradstreet, General John, 48, 57, 58
British Army: at Boston, 74; at Brunswick, 109; at Bunker-Hill, 72; at Charles-Town, 71, 72, 74; infantry of, 72; light-horse of, 98; at Long-Island, 87; occupation of New-York, 111; outrages by, 104, 117; reinforcement of, 113; respect for Continentals, 91; respect for Putnam, 118; in Seven Years' War, 20, 27, 30, 38, 53–55; size of, 89, 92; at Trenton, 100; on York Island, 8n, 9n, 120
British Navy: in East-River, 88; provisioning of, 80; reinforcement of, 82; at Ticonderoga, 22
British Regulars (Seven Years' War), 20, 30
Brown, Captain, 96n
Buchanan, Captain, 116
Bunker-Hill, battle of, 71–74, 75, 91, 94; Putnam at, 73
Burgoyne, General John: reduction of Ticonderoga, 110; surrender of, 115
Bushnell, David, 82, 84, 87n

Camp-making, in Seven Years' War, 20–21
Canada, reduction of, 53
Carthagena, 57
Charles-Town, British possession of, 71, 72, 74
Chasseurs, German, 95, 100
Chastelleux, Marquis de, 8n, 11n
Chester, Captain Thomas, 72
Cincinnati, Society of: in Connecticut, x, 1, 127; founding of, xxi, 2
Cincinnatus, x–xi
Clear River, 41
Clinton, General James, 115
Clinton, Governor George, 114, 115; at West-Point, 120
Clinton, Sir Henry, 114–15
Cochnawaga warriors, 57; village of, 55
Connecticut: Stamp Act in, 60–61; State troops, 10n
Connecticut brigade, mutiny of, xviii–xix, 121–22
Connecticut General Assembly, xix, 121; promotion of Putnam, 25; Putnam in, 59
Connecticut Wits, ix–x
Constitution, U. S., 132–34, 138; adoption of, 134–35; threats to, 135–36
Constitutional Convention, 132, 134
Continental Army, xvii–xviii; battle standard of, 76–77; brigades of, 88, 110–11, 121; British respect for, 91; character of, 70; Congress's policy toward, xviii, 93, 130; defence of New-York city, 78;

discipline in, 70, 88, 90, 93, 96; dissolution of, 2; ingratitude toward, xviii–xxi, 125; levies in, 88, 110; militias' aid to, 113; provisioning of, xviii, 70; at Red Hook, 80; secrets in, 11n; sickness in, 90
Continental Congress: Declaration of the Causes and Necessities of Taking up Arms, 76; formation of, 59–60; inquiry into military disasters, 120; military policy of, xviii, 93, 130; weakness of, 134, 138
Cooper, James Fenimore, xii
Cop's Hill (Boston), 71
Cornwallis, Lord Charles, 100, 101, 106n; foraging parties of, 108
Cow-boys (irregulars), 117
Crosswick's, New Jersey: Putnam at, 101
Crown-Point, New York: in Seven Years' War, 19, 25, 53
Cuban campaign, 56–57
Cultural memory, xiv
Currency, fluctuations in, 128–29

D'Auberteiul, 6n
Davis, Major John, 107
Declaration of the Causes and Necessities of Taking up Arms (Continental Congress), 76
Declaration of Rights and Grievances (Stamp Act Congress), 60
Delancey, Colonel James, 116–17
Delancey, General Oliver, 116

D'Ell, Captain, 37, 41–42, 43, 44;
death of, 57–58
Demolition machine, Bushnell's,
82–87
Detroit, siege of, 57–58
Dickenson, General Philemon,
105n, 106
Dictator, xi
Dieskau, Baron Ludwig August,
20
Dryden, John, xiii
Dubois, Colonel, 115
Durkee, Lieutenant Robert, 20,
21; in Revolution, 33n; in
South-Bay expedition, 33
Dwight, Timothy, x
Dyer, Thomas Henry, xi

Eagle (gunship), 85
East Chester, Connecticut, 10n
East-River, British fleet in, 88
Education: colonial, 11–12; in
Federalist era, 136
Erskine, Sir William, 85n
Esopus, burning of, 115

Fabius Cunctator, Washington
as, 91–92
Farms, devastation of, 96
Federal government: adoption
of, 132; principles of, 133–35;
threats to, 131–32, 135–36
Federalists, Republican ideals of,
xix
Fitch, Governor, 61–62
Flatbush, battle of, 87
Foragers, British, 106, 108
Forbes, General John, 39
Forman, Colonel, 100
Fort Dummer, assault on, 49

Fort DuQuesne, capture of, 39
Fort Edward, 22; British troops
at, 27; burning of, 35–36;
strengthening of, 28
Fort Lee, British capture of, 98
Fort Miller, 39–41
Fort Montgomery, 113; Clinton's
attack on, 114–15;
congressional inquiry into,
120; fall of, 119
Fort Oswego, loss of, 24–25
Fort Ticonderoga, 23, 38; British
capture of, 53; British fleet at,
22; Burgoyne's reduction of,
110, 111; Putnam at, 20–21,
23–24, 47; repulse before,
35–39
Fort Washington, 8n, 97; British
capture of, 98
Fort William Henry: fall of, 25,
27–28; siege of, 26
France, aid to Revolution, 128
Freebooters, in West-Chester,
111–12, 116
French Army: casualties of, 23;
Putnam's kindness to, 38
French and Indian War. *See*
Seven Years' War
Frog's Neck, 10n; Howe at, 97
Frontenac, capture of, 48

Gage, General Thomas: at
Concord, 66; Putnam's talks
with, 64, 67n
Gardiner, Mrs. (second wife of
Putnam), 14
Germaine, Lord George, 106n
Gladwine, Major, 58
Golden age, American, xvi, 14
Goldsmith, Oliver, xi

Governor's Island, submarine
machine at, 87
Great Britain: treaty with
Indians, 58; war with Spain,
55–56. *See also* British Army;
British Navy
Greene, General Nathaniel:
brigades of, 88; illness of, 87,
89
Gurney, Colonel, 107

Half-Way-Brook, skirmish at,
21–22
Harlaem Heights: battle of, 94–
96; patriots' occupation of,
89–90
Harman, Captain, 43, 44
Hartford, 60–61, 121
Havannah expedition, 56–57;
prize money for, 62
Haviland, Colonel: at Fort
Edward, 35–36; in Havannah
expedition, 57n
Hazen's infantry, 121
Heath, General William, 8n,
9n, 88; defence of New-York,
78
Hessians, 98, 99; at Harlaem
Heights, 95; at Long-Island,
87; at Trenton, 100
Hog Island, 70
Hopkinson, Francis: *The Battle
of the Kegs*, 83n–87n
Horn's Hook, 89
Horse-Neck, Connecticut, 122
Howe, Admiral Richard, 85
Howe, Lord George: death of,
37; at Ticonderoga, 36
Howe, Mrs.: captivity of, 48–52;
children of, 49–50, 51, 52, 53;

Putnam's aid to, 52–53;
Schuyler's aid to, 51–52
Howe, Sir William, 84n; at
battle of Harlaem Heights, 95,
97; at Bunker-Hill, 71;
campaign of 1777, 110;
cantonments of, 106–7;
invasion of Pennsylvania, 111;
troop strength of, 89, 92
Hudson River, defence of, 78, 115
Humphreys, David, 123; career
of, ix; first-person perspective
of, xv; at Fort Montgomery,
114n; *On the Happiness of
America*, xiv; at Harlaem
Heights, 89–90; literary
output of, x; *Oration on the
Political Situation of the United
States*, xxi, 127–140; in
Philadelphia, 97; service under
Washington, ix, xv, 9n–10n;
sources of, 8; use of fable, xii,
xiii

Independence, anniversary
celebrations of, 127
Indians: capture of Mrs. Howe,
49; capture of Putnam, 43–47;
casualties among, 23; at fall of
Fort William Henry, 27–28; at
Fort Miller, 40–41; runners,
30–31; torture of Putnam, 45–
46; treaty with Britain, 58;
wars with Britain, 57–58
Individual rights, and individual
interests, xix–xx
Ingersol (stamp-master), 60–61n
Intelligence gathering, 112;
Putnam's, 101; in Seven Years'
War, 24; Washington on, 105n

Johnson, Sir William: defeat of
Dieskau, 20; relief of Fort
William Henry, 27

Kegs (demolition devices), 82n
King's-bridge, New York, 97;
British at, 98
Knowlton, Captain, 72
Knowlton, Lieutenant-Colonel
Thomas, 94; death of, 96n

Ladd, Dr., 7
La Fayette, Marquis de, 8n
Lake George, in Seven Years'
War, 22–23, 36, 39
La Radiere, Colonel, 119–20
Lawrence's Neck, British
redoubt at, 108
Lee, Colonel Henry, 123
Lee, Major-General Charles, 74;
capture of, 98; defence of
New-York city, 77, 78
Leitch, Major, 94, 95n
Levies, in Continental Army, 88,
110
Lexington, battle of, 66–67
Light-horse, British, 98
Little, Captain, 28, 29
Livy, xi
Long-Island: battle of, 88;
Putnam at, 87–88
Loudon, Earl of, 25, 26
Louisbourg, in Seven Years'
War, 25, 26, 39
Loyalists. *See* Tories
Lyman, General Phineas, 28, 29,
35; death of, 63; in England,
62
Lyman's regiment
(Connecticut), 18

M'Fingal (Trumbull), x, 67n–
68n
M'Pherson, Captain, 102–3
Marriage, colonial, 13
Massachusetts: alteration of
charter, 63; brigades of, 110–11
Meigs, Colonel R. J., 114, 116;
regiment of, 112
Mifflin, Colonel Thomas, 78
Militia, 88; aid to Continental
Army, 113; versus standing
army, 93; training of, 66
Minutemen, training of, 66
Mississippi, land grant in, 62–63
Mohawks, 31
Molang (partizan), 34, 42; rescue
of Putnam, 46
Monongahela River, in Seven
Years' War, 20
Monro, Colonel, 26, 27
Montcalm, Marquis de, 26–27;
examination of Putnam, 47
Montreal, British campaign
against, 53–55
Morris-Town, Washington at,
101, 102
Mount-Holly, New Jersey, 100
Mount Washington, New York,
89
Murray, General James, 53–55
Myth, social use of, xiv, xv

Nelson, Colonel, 108
New-Hampshire brigade, 110,
121
New-Haven, yeoman's march
on, 60
New-Rochelle, Putnam at, 116
Newspapers, American, 118–19
New-York brigade, 110–11

New-York city: British
occupation of, 111; fortification
of, 77–82, 92; Lee's defence of,
77; patriots' evacuation of, 97;
Provisional Congress of, 82
Noddle-island, 70
North-Carolina, 135n
North-River, 114

Officers, Provincial: land grant
for, 62–63
Oswegatchie, attack on, 54–55
The Ovens, Putnam at, 20–21
"Owish" (Mohawk word), 31, 32

Palmer, Lieutenant Nathan, 113
Parsons, General Samuel
Holden, 87n, 114, 119
Patriotism, xix
Peek's-Kill, New York, 113
Pennsylvania, Howe's invasion
of, 111
Percy, Lord Hugh, 64, 66
Philadelphia, Putnam in, 97, 98–
100
Pitcairne, Major John, 73
Plutarch, xiii
Pope, Miss (first wife of
Putnam), 14
Princeton: battle of, 102–3;
Putnam at, xviii, 101–3, 107–
9; Washington at, 101
Property, devastation of, 96, 104
Provincial troops (Seven Years'
War), 20, 34; at Ticonderoga,
38, 39
Putnam, Captain Joseph, 11
Putnam, Daniel, 123
Putnam, Israel, 69; aid to
civilians, 118; aid to Mrs.

Howe, 52–53; athleticism of,
13; back pay of, xx, 125; in
Boston, 71; at Bunker-Hill, 73;
in burning of Fort Edward,
35–36; capture by Indians, xii,
43–47, 55; capture of French
prisoner, 4; character of, 2, 12–
13, 118; as Cincinnatus, xi–xiv,
xvi; commands of, 18–20, 74,
87–88, 110, 112–20; and
Connecticut brigade mutiny,
xviii–xix, 121–22; in
Connecticut General
Assembly, 59; correspondence
of, 12, 107n, 108n; at
Crosswick's, 101; death of, 126;
disobedience to orders, 29–30;
education of, 12; erroneous
accounts of, 7–8, 9; execution
of spy, 113; at fall of Fort
William Henry, 28; family of,
11, 14; farming by, 14, 17–18, 59,
62; at Fort Edward, 29–30;
fortification of New-York, 77–
82; fortification of
Philadelphia, 97, 98–100;
fortification of West-Point,
119–20, 123; at Fort Miller,
39–41; at Fort William Henry,
25–26; General Orders of,
79n, 99n; at Harlaem Heights,
89–90, 96; in Havannah
campaign, 56; at Horse-Neck,
122; illnesses of, xix, 99, 123;
imprisonment by French, 27,
47–48; kindness to enemy, 38;
at Lake George, 22–23;
military ruses of, 103; in
Mississippi expedition, 62–63;
Mohawk scouts of, 31;

Molang's rescue of, 46; in Montreal campaign, 54–55; in New Jersey, 97; at New-Rochelle, 116; at outbreak of War, 66; in Pomfret, 14; at Princeton, xviii, 101–3, 107–9; promotion to major, 25; Rangers of, 30; at Reading, 121; release from captivity, 48; retirement from Seven Years' War, 59; versus Rogers, 42; shipwreck of, 56; in South-Bay expedition, 31–35; and Stamp Act, 61–62; and submarine machine, 87; surveillance of French, 41; at Ticonderoga, 20–21, 23, 36–39; torture by Indians, 45–46; on war with Britain, 64–66; Washington's correspondence with, xx, 77–79, 99–100, 109–10, 119, 124–26; wives of, 14; wolf hunt of, 14–17

Putnam, John, 11

Quebec, conquest of, 53

Rangers: Knowlton's, 94; Putnam's, 30
Reading, Massachusetts, 121
Red Hook, fortification of, 80
Refugees, Tory, 108
Religion, in American republic, 140
Revolution, American: commencement of, 66–67; events preceding, 63–64; financing of, 128–31; Republican ideals of, xix
Rhode-Island, 135n

Rhode-Island brigade, 111
Rivington, James, 118–19
Robertson, General, 118–19
Rogers, Major Robert, 18–19; at Fort Edward, 29; at Lake George, 22–23; surveillance of French, 41; at Ticonderoga, 38; at Wood-Creek, 41, 42
Roman republic, America as, x, xi, xix
Root, Colonel, 114

Sabbath-Day-Point, rencounter at, 22
Schuyler, Colonel Peter, 47; aid to Mrs. Howe, 51–52; release from captivity, 48
Separation of powers, in government, 133–34
Seven Years' War: British army in, 20, 27, 30, 38, 53–55; Crown-Point in, 19, 25, 53; encampments of, 20–21; intelligence gathering in, 24; Lake George in, 22–23, 36, 39; Louisbourg in, 25, 26, 39; Monongahela in, 20; outbreak of, 18; Provincial troops in, 20, 34, 38, 39; Putnam's retirement from, 59; Ticonderoga in 20–24, 35–39, 47, 53
Shays's Rebellion, xxi
Sheldon's regiment, 10n, 121
Sheriff, Colonel, 64
Shirley, General William, 24
Skinner's brigade, 108
Small, Colonel, 64, 73
Smith, Lieutenant-Colonel Francis, 66
Smith, Major, 108–9

South-Bay, expedition to, 31–35
South-Carolina, patriot fleet at, 77
Spain, war with Britain, 55–56
Speculation, in currency, 129
Spencer, Brigadier General, 81, 88; at Harlaem Heights, 89, 96
Spies: British, 113; Putnam's use of, 101
St. John's, Mrs. Howe at, 50–51
St. Lawrence River, 54
Stamp Act, 59–61; repeal of, 62
Stark, General John, 8n
Staten Island, British at, 80, 87
Stiles, Yale President Ezra, 87n
Stirling, Brigadier-General Lord, 81, 105n; imprisonment of, 88
Stockton, Major Richard, 108
Stony-Point, 123
Submarine machine, Bushnell's, 82–87
Sullivan, General John, 78, 88
Sutton, Betsey, 117–18
Sutton, William, 117
Symmonds, Commodore, 82n

Tories, xvi, 111, 112; depredations by, 111; disposal of property from, 118; Putnam's actions against, 108
Treaty of Paris (1763), 57
Treaty of Paris (1783), xx
Trenton, Washington at, 10n, 98
Trumbull, Colonel Joseph, 78n
Trumbull, John (painter), 73
Trumbull, John (poet), *M'Fingal*, x, 67n–68n

Tryon, Governor William, 113, 116, 122
Turtle Bay, British landing at, 89

Union, threats to, 132, 134
United States: Congress of, 133; Constitution, 132–36, 138; destiny of, 137–39; geographical advantages of, 138–39; individual interests in, xx, 129; revolutionary ideals of, 131–32; separation of powers in, 133–34; virtue of citizens, 136–37, 140; wartime government of, 129. *See also* Continental Congress; Federal government

Vandeput, Captain, 80
Van Tassel, Mr., 116
Vaughan, General, 115
Veterans, Revolutionary: grievances of, xx–xxi; pay for, 130–31
Virtus, x; in American society, xvi, 136–37; in Humphreys's *Oration*, xxi; in *Life of Putnam*, xvii, 1
The Vision of Columbus (Barlow), x, 8n, 73–74

Wadsworth, Jeremiah, xi, 1, 123
Waldo, Dr. Albigence, xii–xiii, xiv, 8n
Ward, Major General Artemas, 74
Warner, General Seth, 105n
Warren, General Joseph, 71; death of, 72, 73, 74n

Washington, George, 8n;
confidence in army, 96;
correspondence with Putnam,
xx, 77–79, 99–100, 109–10,
119, 124–26; crossing of
Delaware, 100; as Fabius
Cunctator, 91–92; at Harlaem
Heights, 89, 95–96;
Humphreys's service to, ix, xv,
9n; on intelligence gathering,
105n; lieutenants of, 74;
military ruses of, 90–91, 101;
at Morris-Town, 101, 102; in
New-York city, 81; occupation
of Boston, 77; on permanent
army, 93–94; presidency of,
xxi, 140; at Princeton, 101;
Public Orders of, 95n–96n;
retreat from New-York, 98, 99
Webb, General, 21–22, 23, 27; at
Fort William Henry, 25–26

Weedon's regiment, 94
West-Chester, Connecticut, 10n;
freebooters in, 111–12, 116
West-Point, fortification of, 119–
20, 123
Whigs, xvi; plundering of
Tories, 111
White-Plains, battle of, 120
Wioming, battle of, 33n
Wolfe, General James: at
Louisbourg, 39; Montreal
campaign of, 53
Wolf hunt, Putnam's, 14–17
Wood-Creek, rencounters at, 32,
34, 41–43
Wyllys, Colonel, 114n

York Island, British on, 8n,
9n, 120
Yorktown, surrender at, ix,
111n

This book is set in Adobe Caslon. Drawn in 1990 by Carol Twombly, it is based on faces cut in the 1720s and '30s by the English type founder and designer William Caslon. A sturdy face possessed of great charm and simplicity, Calson was the first typeface to be used in the American colonies. Revolutionary War broadsides, including the Declaration of Independence, and the first books printed in America were set in Caslon.

Printed on paper that is acid-free and meets the requirements of the American National Standard for Permanence of Paper for Printed Library Materials, z39.48-1992. ♾

Book design by Sandra Strother Hudson, Athens, Georgia
Typography by Impressions Book and Journal Services, Inc.,
Madison, Wisconsin
Hardcovers printed by Thomson-Shore, Inc.,
Dexter, Michigan, and bound by
John H. Dekker & Sons, Inc., Grand Rapids, Michigan
Paperbacks printed and bound by Thomson-Shore, Inc.,
Dexter, Michigan